Urban Green Space Usage and Nature Satisfaction

This book provides an analysis of nature satisfaction, nature relatedness, and the motivations for using urban green spaces. It explores the use of spaces such as parks, waterfronts, wooded areas, and fields among different life course phases and socio-economic classes.

Through a detailed analysis of primary data from two major German cities, Cologne and Hamburg, the book examines the availability, use, and satisfaction with urban green spaces and provides insights into the predictors of nature satisfaction in an urban context. The book also combines the subjective assessments of the respondents with objective data. It considers the varying reliance on urban green spaces due to the availability of private green spaces and individual nature relatedness. It provides insights on the needs of different population groups in cities, providing a scientific basis for improving or implementing green space planning approaches.

This book will be of interest to researchers in sociology, urban studies, public health, environmental studies, and human geography.

Tetiana Dovbischuk is Research Associate at the Chair of Ecologisation and Quantitative Methods of Social Research at the University of Hamburg, Germany.

Urban Green Space Usage and Nature Satisfaction

Across Life Course Phases and Socio-Economic Classes

Tetiana Dovbischuk

LONDON AND NEW YORK

First published 2025
by Routledge
4 Park Square, Milton Park, Abingdon, Oxon OX14 4RN

and by Routledge
605 Third Avenue, New York, NY 10158

Routledge is an imprint of the Taylor & Francis Group, an informa business

© 2025 Tetiana Dovbischuk

The right of Tetiana Dovbischuk to be identified as author of this work has been asserted in accordance with sections 77 and 78 of the Copyright, Designs and Patents Act 1988.

All rights reserved. No part of this book may be reprinted or reproduced or utilised in any form or by any electronic, mechanical, or other means, now known or hereafter invented, including photocopying and recording, or in any information storage or retrieval system, without permission in writing from the publishers.

Trademark notice: Product or corporate names may be trademarks or registered trademarks, and are used only for identification and explanation without intent to infringe.

British Library Cataloguing-in-Publication Data
A catalogue record for this book is available from the British Library

ISBN: 978-1-032-90098-8 (hbk)
ISBN: 978-1-032-90100-8 (pbk)
ISBN: 978-1-003-54614-6 (ebk)

DOI: 10.4324/9781003546146

Typeset in Times New Roman
by Apex CoVantage, LLC

Contents

Acknowledgements

I would like to thank my doctoral supervisor, Stefanie Kley, for her valuable guidance, and my student assistant, Talea Bruns, for her strong support in preparing the results. I would also like to thank the German Research Foundation (DFG) for funding this project under project number 430171901.

Tables

Figures

Abbreviations

CATI	Computer-Assisted Telephone Interviewing
CAWI	Computer-Assisted Web Interviewing
CNS	Connectedness to Nature Scale
DFG	German Research Foundation
EGP	Erikson–Goldthorpe–Portocarero (scheme)
GESIS	Gesellschaft Sozialwissenschaftlicher Infrastruktureinrichtungen e.V.
IEA	International Association for the Evaluation of Educational Achievement
ISCO08	International Standard Classification of Occupations from 2008
MAXQDA	Max Qualitative Data Analysis
NEP	New Environmental Paradigm (scale)
NR	Nature Relatedness (scale)
QGIS	Quantum Geographic Information System
RDD	Random Digit Dialing
WHO	World Health Organization

Introduction

According to biophilia theory (Kellert & Wilson, 1993; Wilson, 1984), all living beings, including humans, seek closeness to nature and to everything that is vital or alive. Although the genetic potential and cross-cultural applicability of biophilia theory seem to be controversial (cf. Joye & De Block, 2011; Joye & van den Berg, 2011), the author believes that applying this theory to primary data would support nature's ability for stress management (Ulrich et al., 1991) and attention restoration (Kaplan, 1995) in an urban context. One potential explanation for the human tendency towards nature is that urban living is a relatively recent phenomenon in the context of human evolutionary history. Currently, over half of the world's population (United Nations, 2023) and 74% of the German population (Statistisches Bundesamt, 2021) live in cities, with a clear upward trend. The popularity of urban green and water spaces and their positive effects on mental and physical health and well-being (cf. Abraham et al., 2010; Bertram & Rehdanz, 2015; Kley & Dovbischuk, 2021; Krekel et al., 2016) could be attributed to the importance of the aforementioned need for proximity to life forms, as suggested by biophilia theory. Of course, the extent of reliance on urban green spaces depends on the availability of private green spaces, such as gardens. In addition, individual connectedness to nature (Mayer & Frantz, 2004; Nisbet et al., 2009) varies from person to person and should be taken into account.

The aim of this book is to analyse the usage preferences for urban green spaces among different population groups, and the relevance of these urban green spaces for the satisfaction of city dwellers with nature. To this end, the book employs two major German cities, Cologne and Hamburg, as a case study. The book begins with an overview of previous research on the relevance of green spaces in residential environments in Chapter 1. Most traditional approaches have concentrated on analysing the relationship between greenery and outcomes such as mental or physical health (cf. Abraham et al., 2010; Coppel & Wüstemann, 2017; Jennings & Bamkole, 2019; Stigsdotter et al., 2010; Wang et al., 2022) and other sub-areas of well-being (cf. Bertram & Rehdanz, 2015; Chang et al., 2020; Kley & Dovbischuk, 2021;

DOI: 10.4324/9781003546146-1

Krekel et al., 2016; Zhao et al., 2024). In this context, objective statistical data are often used to determine the availability of green spaces in the neighbourhood of the place of residence (cf. Bertram & Rehdanz, 2015; Coppel & Wüstemann, 2017; Krekel et al., 2016; Wang et al., 2022). A comparison of the subjective assessment of green space availability with the objective measurement of green space based on statistical geodata indicates that subjective assessments have a greater influence on well-being (Lee et al., 2016). To date, relatively few attempts have been made to analyse the relevance of green spaces across different life course phases (Douglas et al., 2017) or socio-economic classes.

Chapter 2 then provides an overview of the conceptual considerations underlying the choice of research method and a methodological description of its implementation. A precise questionnaire was developed to accurately capture the availability and use of green spaces in and around the respondent's place of residence. This chapter describes how the random sample was conducted in the cities of Cologne and Hamburg, why these cities were chosen, and whether the sample is representative for these cities.

Chapter 3 presents the findings of the study on the availability and use of green spaces. It analyses the importance of different types of green spaces for different life course phases and socio-economic classes. A distinction is made among parks, waterfronts, woodlands, and fields in cities. This section also examines the extent to which the use of public green spaces differs when urban dwellers do not have their own gardens. It further explores the average duration of visits to these green spaces by the above groups. In addition, objective data based on the geocoded addresses of the respondents are used to compare whether the subjective responses of the respondents and the objective data yield comparable results.

The aim of Chapter 4 is to outline the relevance of nature relatedness in the urban environment. To this end, it first discusses different methodological approaches to measuring nature relatedness. This is followed by an analysis of nature relatedness across different life course phases and socio-economic classes within the sample.

Chapter 5 focuses on analysing important aspects that influence nature satisfaction in urban areas, and the extent of differences across life course phases and socio-economic classes. To date, there have been comparatively few attempts to investigate the precise predictors that contribute to satisfaction with nature (Kearney, 2006; Qiao et al., 2021; Wu et al., 2019). To the best of the author's knowledge, there is no published work that examines the availability of different types of neighbourhood green spaces and their impact on nature satisfaction, particularly with regard to differences across life course phases or socio-economic classes.

Finally, Chapter 6 briefly summarises the findings and offers some concluding remarks.

References

Abraham, A., Sommerhalder, K., & Abel, T. (2010). Landscape and well-being: A scoping study on the health-promoting impact of outdoor environments. *International Journal of Public Health, 55*(1), 59–69. https://doi.org/10.1007/s00038-009-0069-z

Bertram, C., & Rehdanz, K. (2015). The role of urban green space for human well-being. *Ecological Economics, 120*, 139–152. https://doi.org/10.1016/j.ecolecon.2015.10.013

Chang, C.-C., Oh, R. R. Y., Nghiem, T. P. L., Zhang, Y., Tan, C. L. Y., Lin, B. B., Gaston, K. J., Fuller, R. A., & Carrasco, L. R. (2020). Life satisfaction linked to the diversity of nature experiences and nature views from the window. *Landscape and Urban Planning, 202*, 103874. https://doi.org/10.1016/j.landurbplan.2020.103874

Coppel, G., & Wüstemann, H. (2017). The impact of urban green space on health in Berlin, Germany: Empirical findings and implications for urban planning. *Landscape and Urban Planning, 167*, 410–418. https://doi.org/10.1016/j.landurbplan.2017.06.015

Douglas, O., Lennon, M., & Scott, M. (2017). Green space benefits for health and well-being: A life-course approach for urban planning, design and management. *Cities, 66*, 53–62. https://doi.org/10.1016/j.cities.2017.03.011

Jennings, V., & Bamkole, O. (2019). The relationship between social cohesion and urban green space: An avenue for health promotion. *International Journal of Environmental Research and Public Health, 16*(3), 452. https://doi.org/10.3390/ijerph16030452

Joye, Y., & De Block, A. (2011). 'Nature and I are two': A critical examination of the biophilia hypothesis. *Environmental Values, 20*(2), 189–215. https://doi.org/10.3197/096327111x12997574391724

Joye, Y., & van den Berg, A. (2011). Is love for green in our genes? A critical analysis of evolutionary assumptions in restorative environments research. *Urban Forestry & Urban Greening, 10*(4), 261–268. https://doi.org/10.1016/j.ufug.2011.07.004

Kaplan, S. (1995). The restorative benefits of nature: Toward an integrative framework. *Journal of Environmental Psychology, 15*(3), 169–182. https://doi.org/10.1016/0272-4944(95)90001-2

Kearney, A. R. (2006). Residential development patterns and neighborhood satisfaction. *Environment and Behavior, 38*(1), 112–139. https://doi.org/10.1177/0013916505277607

Kellert, S., & Wilson, E. (1993). *The biophilia hypothesis*. Island Press.

Kley, S., & Dovbischuk, T. (2021). How a lack of green in the residential environment lowers the life satisfaction of city dwellers and increases their willingness to relocate. *Sustainability, 13*(7), 3984. https://doi.org/10.3390/su13073984

Krekel, C., Kolbe, J., & Wüstemann, H. (2016). The greener, the happier? The effect of urban land use on residential well-being. *Ecological Economics, 121*, 117–127. https://doi.org/10.1016/j.ecolecon.2015.11.005

Lee, S. M., Conway, T. L., Frank, L. D., Saelens, B. E., Cain, K. L., & Sallis, J. F. (2016). The relation of perceived and objective environment attributes to neighborhood satisfaction. *Environment and Behavior*, *49*(2), 136–160. https://doi.org/10.1177/0013916515623823

Mayer, F. S., & Frantz, C. M. (2004). The connectedness to nature scale: A measure of individuals' feeling in community with nature. *Journal of Environmental Psychology*, *24*(4), 503–515. https://doi.org/10.1016/j.jenvp.2004.10.001

Nisbet, E. K., Zelenski, J. M., & Murphy, S. A. (2009). The nature relatedness scale. *Environment and Behavior*, *41*(5), 715–740. https://doi.org/10.1177/0013916508318748

Qiao, Y., Chen, Z., Chen, Y., & Zheng, T. (2021). Deciphering the link between mental health and green space in Shenzhen, China: The mediating impact of residents' satisfaction. *Frontiers in Public Health*, *9*, 561809. https://doi.org/10.3389/fpubh.2021.561809

Statistisches Bundesamt. (2021). *Städte (alle Gemeinden mit Stadtrecht) nach Fläche, Bevölkerung und Bevölkerungsdichte am 31.12.2020*. www.destatis.de/DE/Themen/Laender-Regionen/Regionales/Gemeindeverzeichnis/Administrativ/05-staedte.html

Stigsdotter, U. K., Ekholm, O., Schipperijn, J., Toftager, M., Kamper-Jorgensen, F., & Randrup, T. B. (2010). Health promoting outdoor environments – associations between green space, and health, health-related quality of life and stress based on a Danish national representative survey. *Scandinavian Journal of Public Health*, *38*(4), 411–417. https://doi.org/10.1177/1403494810367468

Ulrich, R., Simons, R., Losito, B., Fiorito, E., Miles, M., & Zelson, M. (1991). Stress recovery during exposure to natural and urban environments. *Journal of Environmental Psychology*, *11*, 201–230. https://doi.org/10.1016/S0272-4944(05)80184-7

United Nations. (2023). *The sustainable development goals report (Special edition: Towards a Rescue Plan for People and Planet)*. https://unstats.un.org/sdgs/report/2023/The-Sustainable-Development-Goals-Report-2023.pdf

Wang, R., Feng, Z., & Pearce, J. (2022). Neighbourhood greenspace quantity, quality and socioeconomic inequalities in mental health. *Cities*, *129*. https://doi.org/10.1016/j.cities.2022.103815

Wilson, E. O. (1984). *Biophilia*. Harvard University Press. www.degruyter.com/document/doi/10.4159/9780674045231/html

Wu, W. J., Wang, M., Zhu, N., Zhang, W. Y., & Sun, H. (2019). Residential satisfaction about urban greenness: Heterogeneous effects across social and spatial gradients. *Urban Forestry & Urban Greening*, *38*, 133–144. https://doi.org/10.1016/j.ufug.2018.11.011

Zhao, Y., van den Berg, P. E. W., Ossokina, I. V., & Arentze, T. A. (2024). How do urban parks, neighborhood open spaces, and private gardens relate to individuals' subjective well-being: Results of a structural equation model. *Sustainable Cities and Society*, *101*, 105094. https://doi.org/10.1016/j.scs.2023.105094

1 Beneficial effects of residential greenery in urban context

Compared to urban environments, green, natural environments have consistently more positive effects on overall well-being and its sub-domains. MacKerron and Mourato (2013) found that people are significantly happier in green surroundings than in built-up urban environments, using data from a self-created geo-supported smartphone application.[1] Mayer et al. (2009) observed that spending time in nature led to significantly more positive emotions than spending time in the city. When investigating the restorative properties of preferred locations, Korpela et al. (2001) showed that natural environments account for a substantial proportion of pleasant places while urban places account for a considerable proportion of unpleasant ones. Lindal and Hartig (2015) emphasise the role of green spaces in influencing the likelihood of attentional recovery, showing that streetscapes with more greenery have a higher probability of attentional recovery than urban streetscapes with little or no greenery. Similarly, Taylor and Kuo (2009) found that children with attention deficits were able to concentrate better after walking in a park than after walking in an urban environment. In terms of residential satisfaction, Kweon et al. (2010) found that trees contribute positively to neighbourhood satisfaction, while buildings have the opposite effect. In a study of health benefits and recovery after surgery, Ulrich (1984) found that patients recovering in a hospital room with a view of nature from the window recovered faster than those with a view of a built urban environment.

The positive influence of natural environments is often attributed to the theory of biophilia (Kellert & Wilson, 1993). This theory suggests that humans instinctively seek proximity to nature, particularly in urban environments, which are relatively recent in human evolution. Biophilia theory emphasises humans' innate affinity with natural elements and suggests that contact with nature promotes well-being and the ability to regenerate. In the field of urban design, biophilia theory has been criticised because it is argued that not only evolutionary but also cultural development should be considered, as some people might prefer a mix of natural and urban elements (Joye & De Block, 2011; Joye & van den Berg, 2011). It is therefore important to analyse how much nature urban dwellers need, and whether their own affinity with

DOI: 10.4324/9781003546146-2

nature, such as nature relatedness (Nisbet et al., 2009, see also Chapter 4), plays a role. However, there seems to be a consensus that natural spaces provide opportunities for stress recovery (Groenewegen et al., 2012; Stigsdotter et al., 2010; Ulrich et al., 1991) and attention restoration (Taylor & Kuo, 2009; Honold et al., 2016; Kaplan, 1995, 2001; Korpela et al., 2001; Lindal & Hartig, 2015; van den Berg et al., 2010). Especially in the urban context, which is characterised by numerous stressors such as noise (Diekmann et al., 2023; Park & Evans, 2016; Preisendörfer et al., 2022), air pollution (Best & Rüttenauer, 2018; Wolch et al., 2014), high traffic volumes (Diekmann et al., 2023; Preisendörfer et al., 2022), overcrowding (Park & Evans, 2016), and vulnerability to crisis situations (Grima et al., 2020; Refisch et al., 2024), natural spaces play a crucial role, as they serve as places where city dwellers can calm down, reduce anxiety and stress, and recharge their energy.

Green spaces and well-being outcomes

Previous research has shown that as the distance from home to the nearest green space increases, *overall health* declines (Coppel & Wüstemann, 2017; Stigsdotter et al., 2010). According to the World Health Organization (WHO), urban green spaces reduce health risks by providing opportunities for stress reduction and relaxation or physical activity while using them (World Health Organization, 2017). By providing opportunities for stress restoration (Taylor & Kuo, 2009; Groenewegen et al., 2012; Kaplan, 1995; Korpela et al., 2001; Ulrich et al., 1991; van den Berg et al., 2010; White et al., 2013) and physical activity (Cervero & Duncan, 2003; Coombes et al., 2010; de Jong et al., 2012; Kim & Miller, 2019), green spaces appear to be beneficial for both mental and physical health (see Abraham et al., 2010, for an overview; De Vries et al., 2003; Groenewegen et al., 2012; Hartig et al., 2014; Honold et al., 2016; Jennings & Bamkole, 2019; Maas et al., 2009; Wang et al., 2022). Further studies on health outcomes show that better access to green spaces in urban residential areas is associated with improved behavioural and mental development in children (Bijnens et al., 2020), positive birth outcomes (Hystad et al., 2014), lower probability of being overweight (Coombes et al., 2010; Lovasi et al., 2013) or developing cancer (Demoury et al., 2017), lower likelihood of depression (Cohen-Cline et al., 2015), and even lower mortality (Crouse et al., 2017; James et al., 2016).

Access to green spaces in urban residential areas (Krekel et al., 2016), their amount in the neighbourhood (Bertram & Rehdanz, 2015; Van Herzele & De Vries, 2012; White et al., 2013), individual satisfaction with green spaces in the neighbourhood (Zhao et al., 2024), and looking out of the window at green spaces at home (Chang et al., 2020; Kaplan, 2001; Kley & Dovbischuk, 2021) are associated with better overall *well-being* and higher *life satisfaction*.[2] Additionally, frequent use of green spaces in the neighbourhood (Honold et al., 2016; Ma et al., 2019) and use of not just one but different types of natural spaces (Chang et al., 2020) appear to be associated with higher life satisfaction and well-being.

Van Herzele and De Vries (2012) suggest that the association between neighbourhood greenery and life satisfaction may be mediated by *residential satisfaction*. Indeed, a substantial body of research supports the idea that views of nature from home (Kaplan, 2001; Kearney, 2006; Kley & Dovbischuk, 2024) and the opportunity to visit neighbourhood green spaces (Kearney, 2006; Lee et al., 2016; Van Herzele & De Vries, 2012; Wu et al., 2020; Zhang et al., 2017) are positively associated with residential satisfaction. Analyses of specific neighbourhood landscape components show that even the presence of trees alone in residential streets can increase residential satisfaction (Kweon et al., 2010). Additionally, green spaces also appear to increase place attachment (Arnberger & Eder, 2012; Bonaiuto et al., 1999; Kim & Kaplan, 2004), although it is debatable whether the potential mechanism is not primarily through influencing residential satisfaction (Bonaiuto et al., 1999). Regardless of this, neighbourhood green spaces often serve as places for social interaction and thus promote social cohesion in the neighbourhood (Groenewegen et al., 2012; Jennings & Bamkole, 2019; Kemperman & Timmermans, 2014; Kim & Kaplan, 2004; Maas et al., 2009).

Challenges in measuring green spaces in the neighbourhood

Research on green spaces has used different methods to measure green space availability. These typically include respondents' subjective assessment of the presence or use of local green spaces (Arnberger & Eder, 2012; Chang et al., 2020; Chiesura, 2004; Honold et al., 2016; Kemperman & Timmermans, 2014; Kim & Miller, 2019; Lee et al., 2016; Ma et al., 2019; Refisch et al., 2024; Säumel et al., 2021; Stigsdotter et al., 2010; Van Herzele & De Vries, 2012; Wang et al., 2022; Zhang et al., 2017; Zhao et al., 2024), respondents' subjective ratings of green window views at home (Honold et al., 2016; Kaplan, 2001; Kearney, 2006; Kley & Dovbischuk, 2021, 2024), and – more frequently – objective measurements of green spaces based on respondents' addresses (Astell-Burt et al., 2014; Bertram & Rehdanz, 2015; Bijnens et al., 2020; Cervero & Duncan, 2003; Cohen-Cline et al., 2015; Coombes et al., 2010; Coppel & Wüstemann, 2017; Crouse et al., 2017; de Jong et al., 2012; De Vries et al., 2003; Demoury et al., 2017; Groenewegen et al., 2012; Hystad et al., 2014; James et al., 2016; Kearney, 2006; Kemperman & Timmermans, 2014; Krekel et al., 2016; Kweon et al., 2010; Lee et al., 2016; Lovasi et al., 2013; Maas et al., 2009; van den Berg et al., 2010; Wang et al., 2022; Wei et al., 2023; White et al., 2013; Wu et al., 2020; Zhang et al., 2017). Studies combining these methods are rare (Dovbischuk & Kley, 2024; Honold et al., 2016; Kearney, 2006; Kemperman & Timmermans, 2014;

Kley & Dovbischuk, 2024; Wang et al., 2022). Some studies comparing these measures conclude that they capture similar aspects (Zhang et al., 2017) or that the objective measures of green have less influence on well-being than the respondents' subjective assessments (Dovbischuk & Kley, 2024; Lee et al., 2016). Considering these factors, the current study relies on respondents' subjective assessments of their visits to parks, waterfronts, woodlands, and fields in their neighbourhoods for the majority of the descriptive findings in Chapter 3. In addition, geocoded data on the objective availability of green space are included to assess the validity of the measurement constructs (see the last section of Chapter 3 for more details).

In addition to the studies highlighting the positive effects of access to neighbourhood green spaces, Wu et al. (2020) emphasise the role of the park use over mere availability close to home, showing that park use in particular is positively associated with residential satisfaction. Honold et al. (2016) suggest that the positive association between life satisfaction and green space views from the home window may be influenced by how individuals use their neighbourhood green spaces. Martin et al. (2020) find a positive association between visiting green spaces and general health, while the availability of green spaces does not show a similar relationship. Stigsdotter et al. (2010) find that the reasons for using green spaces vary according to the mental health of residents and that the more frequently green spaces are used, the lower the reported stress levels. Säumel et al. (2021) emphasise the need for research to distinguish between passive and active use of green spaces in residential areas when analysing well-being. While many studies address the frequency of visits to nature (Berdejo-Espinola et al., 2021; Breuste & Artmann, 2020; Chang et al., 2020; Coombes et al., 2010; Grima et al., 2020; Honold et al., 2016; Kearney, 2006; Kemperman & Timmermans, 2014; Kim & Miller, 2019; Ma et al., 2019; Mak & Jim, 2019; Martin et al., 2020; Säumel et al., 2021; Stigsdotter et al., 2010; Zhao et al., 2024), the motivations and reasons for using green spaces receive less scientific attention (with exceptions in Breuste & Artmann, 2020; Chiesura, 2004; Grima et al., 2020; Jensen & Koch, 2004; Kim & Miller, 2019; Lachowycz et al., 2012; Mak & Jim, 2019; Pinto et al., 2021; Refisch et al., 2024; Säumel et al., 2021; Stigsdotter et al., 2010; Tinsley et al., 2002; Zhao et al., 2024). As it is important to capture both the frequency of and the motivations for using green spaces, this work aims to further analyse the identified reasons for using parks, waterfronts, woods, and fields in residential areas within cities in more detail (see Chapter 3).

Green space benefits across life course phases

Urban green spaces should not be analysed as if they are all the same (cf. Breuste & Artmann, 2020), but at least a distinction should be made among urban parks, waterfronts, woods, and fields, as in the present work. Attention should also be paid to whether these green spaces provide similar benefits or are used in comparable ways at different stages of the life course. This question is inspired by the changing dynamics of individual experiences and behaviours over time (Bernardi et al., 2019), which could also be reflected in nature use and its positive effects. The use of a differentiated perspective through a life course approach provides an important policy basis for the development of inclusive urban green spaces, which could take into account the different nature needs in different life course phases.

Indeed, there is evidence that green spaces have different effects on health and well-being across the life course. For example, a recent review by Douglas et al. (2017) recognises the importance of looking at the benefits and use preferences of green spaces separately for different phases of the life course. This review summarises research findings that focus on specific phases of childhood, adolescence, adulthood, or later life. However, it lacks a comparative perspective on the benefits and uses of green spaces at different stages of the life course.

While existing research often examines the effects of green spaces on health and well-being at specific stages of the life course or conducts analyses that do not distinguish among life course phases at all, there are examples that show differences in the effects across the life course. For example, green spaces have been found to have a greater impact on the social support for *children and younger adults* than at other stages of the life course (Maas et al., 2009). In terms of health outcomes, men in *early and middle adulthood* have been shown to benefit more from higher levels of green space (Astell-Burt et al., 2014). Furthermore, the positive relationship between living in a green environment and overall well-being, health, and social support is somewhat stronger for *older adults*, as they have more frequent contact with the local environment compared to other life course phases (De Vries et al., 2003; Krekel et al., 2016; Maas et al., 2009). Based on these findings, this analysis distinguishes among four life course phases: the young adult phase, the family phase, the midlife phase, and the senior phase, as it is assumed that both patterns of nature use and preferences for green spaces differ in these life course phases (more on this in Chapters 3–5)

Social class disparities in green space benefits and usage

There may also be differences across social classes: first, in access to green spaces; second, in the ways in which the upper and lower classes can benefit from them; and third, in the use of green spaces in their neighbourhoods. First, analyses of the Anglo-Saxon context (Wolch et al., 2005, 2014) have demonstrated an unequal distribution of urban green spaces in cities. Instead, German research seems to focus more on analysing the unequal distribution of so-called 'environmental bads', such as air pollution and exposure to residential noise (Best & Rüttenauer, 2018; Diekmann et al., 2023; Preisendörfer et al., 2022), rather than 'environmental goods', such as green spaces. The scientific debate on the unequal distribution of positive environmental goods and negative environmental bads is often conducted under the aspect of environmental justice. The favourable environmental goods, such as the provision of recreational areas and green spaces, are mainly found in affluent and cultivated urban areas. In contrast, the unfavourable environmental bads, such as landfills and major roads, are predominantly found in poor and structurally weak areas (cf. Claßen et al., 2012; Mohai & Saha, 2015). Even in cases where affluent and less affluent neighbourhoods appear to have similar amounts of green space, it is the accessibility of these areas that matters. In a study by Zhang et al. (2017) comparing two Dutch urban neighbourhoods with similar amounts of green space but different socio-economic status, residents of the neighbourhood with the lower socio-economic status had less accessible green space and were less satisfied with their neighbourhood, although overall well-being was not significantly different between the two areas.

Second, lower-class citizens seem to benefit more from green spaces in their neighbourhoods than upper-class citizens (see, e.g. Rigolon et al., 2021 for an overview of health benefits). For example, lower-educated and low-income respondents seem to profit more from living in a green neighbourhood, in terms of both health outcomes (Coppel & Wüstemann, 2017; De Vries et al., 2003; Wang et al., 2022) and residential satisfaction (Kley & Dovbischuk, 2024), while low-income respondents additionally benefit more from green spaces to promote social support (Maas et al., 2009). Among low-income families with preschool children, a higher proportion of trees along residential streets is associated with lower rates of obesity (Lovasi et al., 2013). Additionally, exposure to green space has a greater impact on life expectancy for older adults from low socio-economic backgrounds (Wei et al., 2023).

Third, given the unequal distribution of green space across social classes and the different benefits that green space provides across social classes, it seems possible that patterns of green space use also differ across social classes. In contrast to the more extensively studied differences in use across life course phases (see review by Douglas et al., 2017), there is a notable gap in research on use preferences across social classes. Tinsley et al. (2002) found that there are significant differences in motives for park use across different social milieus among older park users, with social milieu here corresponding to ethnicity rather than socio-economic class.

Notes

1 Built environments are also sometimes perceived as scenic or beautiful and therefore have a positive impact on people's sense of happiness (Seresinhe et al., 2019).

2 However, there is evidence that this relationship might not be linear, as an increasing amount of green space initially increases life satisfaction, but this relationship may reverse after a certain threshold (Bertram & Rehdanz, 2015).

References

Abraham, A., Sommerhalder, K., & Abel, T. (2010). Landscape and well-being: A scoping study on the health-promoting impact of outdoor environments. *International Journal of Public Health, 55*(1), 59–69. https://doi.org/10.1007/s00038-009-0069-z

Arnberger, A., & Eder, R. (2012). The influence of green space on community attachment of urban and suburban residents. *Urban Forestry & Urban Greening, 11*(1), 41–49. https://doi.org/10.1016/j.ufug.2011.11.003

Astell-Burt, T., Mitchell, R., & Hartig, T. (2014). The association between green space and mental health varies across the lifecourse. A longitudinal study. *Journal of Epidemiology and Community Health, 68*(6), 578–583. https://doi.org/10.1136/jech-2013-203767

Berdejo-Espinola, V., Suárez-Castro, A. F., Amano, T., Fielding, K. S., Oh, R. R. Y., & Fuller, R. A. (2021). Urban green space use during a time of stress: A case study during the COVID-19 pandemic in Brisbane, Australia. *People and Nature, 3*(3), 597–609. https://doi.org/10.1002/pan3.10218

Bernardi, L., Huinink, J., & Settersten, R. A. (2019). The life course cube: A tool for studying lives. *Advances in Life Course Research, 41*, 100258. https://doi.org/10.1016/j.alcr.2018.11.004

Bertram, C., & Rehdanz, K. (2015). The role of urban green space for human well-being. *Ecological Economics, 120*, 139–152. https://doi.org/10.1016/j.ecolecon.2015.10.013

Best, H., & Rüttenauer, T. (2018). How selective migration shapes environmental inequality in Germany: Evidence from micro-level panel data. *European Sociological Review, 34*(1), 52–63. https://doi.org/10.1093/esr/jcx082

Bijnens, E. M., Derom, C., Thiery, E., Weyers, S., & Nawrot, T. S. (2020). Residential green space and child intelligence and behavior across urban, suburban, and rural areas in Belgium: A longitudinal birth cohort study of twins. *PLoS Medicine, 17*(8), e1003213. https://doi.org/10.1371/journal.pmed.1003213

Bonaiuto, M., Aiello, A., Perugini, M., Bonnes, M., & Ercolani, A. P. (1999). Multidimensional perception of residential environment quality and neighbourhood attachment in the urban environment. *Journal of Environmental Psychology, 19*(4), 331–352. https://doi.org/10.1006/jevp.1999.0138

Breuste, J., & Artmann, M. (2020). Multi-functional urban green spaces. In J. Breuste, M. Artmann, C. Ioja, & S. Qureshi (Eds.), *Making green cities: Concepts, challenges and practice* (pp. 399–526). Springer.

Cervero, R., & Duncan, M. (2003). Walking, bicycling, and urban landscapes: Evidence from the San Francisco Bay area. *American Journal of Public Health, 93*(9), 1478–1483. https://doi.org/10.2105/ajph.93.9.1478

Chang, C.-C., Oh, R. R. Y., Nghiem, T. P. L., Zhang, Y., Tan, C. L. Y., Lin, B. B., Gaston, K. J., Fuller, R. A., & Carrasco, L. R. (2020). Life satisfaction linked to the diversity of nature experiences and nature views from the window. *Landscape and Urban Planning, 202*, 103874. https://doi.org/10.1016/j.landurbplan.2020.103874

Chiesura, A. (2004). The role of urban parks for the sustainable city. *Landscape and Urban Planning, 68*(1), 129–138. https://doi.org/10.1016/j.landurbplan.2003.08.003

Claßen, T., Heiler, A., & Brei, B. (2012). Urbane Grünräume und gesundheitliche Chancengleichheit -längst nicht alles im "grünen Bereich". In B. E. A. H. Bolte (Ed.), *Umweltgerechtigkeit* (pp. 113–123). Hans Huber.

Cohen-Cline, H., Turkheimer, E., & Duncan, G. E. (2015). Access to green space, physical activity and mental health: A twin study. *Journal of Epidemiology and Community Health*, *69*(6), 523–529. https://doi.org/10.1136/jech-2014-204667

Coombes, E., Jones, A. P., & Hillsdon, M. (2010). The relationship of physical activity and overweight to objectively measured green space accessibility and use. *Social Science & Medicine*, *70*(6), 816–822. https://doi.org/10.1016/j.socscimed.2009.11.020

Coppel, G., & Wüstemann, H. (2017). The impact of urban green space on health in Berlin, Germany: Empirical findings and implications for urban planning. *Landscape and Urban Planning*, *167*, 410–418. https://doi.org/10.1016/j.landurbplan.2017.06.015

Crouse, D. L., Pinault, L., Balram, A., Hystad, P., Peters, P. A., Chen, H., van Donkelaar, A., Martin, R. V., Ménard, R., Robichaud, A., & Villeneuve, P. J. (2017). Urban greenness and mortality in Canada's largest cities: A national cohort study. *The Lancet Planetary Health*, *1*(7), e289–e297. https://doi.org/10.1016/S2542-5196(17)30118-3

de Jong, K., Albin, M., Skärbäck, E., Grahn, P., & Björk, J. (2012). Perceived green qualities were associated with neighborhood satisfaction, physical activity, and general health: Results from a cross-sectional study in suburban and rural Scania, Southern Sweden. *Health & Place*, *18*(6), 1374–1380. https://doi.org/10.1016/j.healthplace.2012.07.001

Demoury, C., Thierry, B., Richard, H., Sigler, B., Kestens, Y., & Parent, M.-E. (2017). Residential greenness and risk of prostate cancer: A case-control study in Montreal, Canada. *Environment International*, *98*, 129–136. https://doi.org/10.1016/j.envint.2016.10.024

De Vries, S., Verheij, R. A., Groenewegen, P. P., & Spreeuwenberg, P. (2003). Natural environments – healthy environments? An exploratory analysis of the relationship between greenspace and health. *Environment and Planning A: Economy and Space*, *35*(10), 1717–1731. https://doi.org/10.1068/a35111

Diekmann, A., Enzler, H. B., Hartmann, J., Kurz, K., Liebe, U., & Preisendörfer, P. (2023). Environmental inequality in four European cities: A study combining household survey and geo-referenced data. *European Sociological Review*, *39*(1), 44–66. https://doi.org/10.1093/esr/jcac028

Douglas, O., Lennon, M., & Scott, M. (2017). Green space benefits for health and well-being: A life-course approach for urban planning, design and management. *Cities*, *66*, 53–62. https://doi.org/10.1016/j.cities.2017.03.011

Dovbischuk, T., & Kley, S. (2024). The call of the green: The role of green spaces in residential relocations across the life course in Germany. *Population, Space and Place*, e2810. https://doi.org/10.1002/psp.2810

Grima, N., Corcoran, W., Hill-James, C., Langton, B., Sommer, H., & Fisher, B. (2020). The importance of urban natural areas and urban ecosystem services during the COVID-19 pandemic. *PLoS One*, *15*(12), e0243344. https://doi.org/10.1371/journal.pone.0243344

Groenewegen, P. P., van den Berg, A. E., Maas, J., Verheij, R. A., & de Vries, S. (2012). Is a green residential environment better for health? If so, why? *Annals of the Association of American Geographers, 102*(5), 996–1003. https://doi.org/10.1080/00045608.2012.674899

Hartig, T., Mitchell, R., De Vries, S., & Frumkin, H. (2014). Nature and health. *Annual Review of Public Health, 35*(1), 207–228. https://doi.org/10.1146/annurev-publhealth-032013-182443

Honold, J., Lakes, T., Beyer, R., & van der Meer, E. (2016). Restoration in urban spaces: Nature views from home, greenways, and public parks. *Environment and Behavior, 48*(6), 796–825. https://doi.org/10.1177/0013916514568556

Hystad, P., Davies, H. W., Frank, L., Van Loon, J., Gehring, U., Tamburic, L., & Brauer, M. (2014). Residential greenness and birth outcomes: Evaluating the influence of spatially correlated built-environment factors. *Environmental Health Perspectives, 122*(10), 1095–1102. https://doi.org/10.1289/ehp.1308049

James, P., Hart, J. E., Banay, R. F., & Laden, F. (2016). Exposure to greenness and mortality in a nationwide prospective cohort study of women. *Environmental Health Perspectives, 124*(9), 1344–1352. https://doi.org/10.1289/ehp.1510363

Jennings, V., & Bamkole, O. (2019). The relationship between social cohesion and urban green space: An avenue for health promotion. *International Journal of Environmental Research and Public Health, 16*(3), 452. https://doi.org/10.3390/ijerph16030452

Jensen, F. S., & Koch, N. E. (2004). Twenty-five years of forest recreation research in Denmark and its influence on forest policy. *Scandinavian Journal of Forest Research, 19*(S4), 93–102.

Joye, Y., & De Block, A. (2011). 'Nature and I are two': A critical examination of the biophilia hypothesis. *Environmental Values, 20*(2), 189–215. https://doi.org/10.3197/096327111x12997574391724

Joye, Y., & van den Berg, A. (2011). Is love for green in our genes? A critical analysis of evolutionary assumptions in restorative environments research. *Urban Forestry & Urban Greening, 10*(4), 261–268. https://doi.org/10.1016/j.ufug.2011.07.004

Kaplan, R. (2001). The nature of the view from home. *Environment and Behavior, 33*(4), 507–542. https://doi.org/10.1177/00139160121973115

Kaplan, S. (1995). The restorative benefits of nature: Toward an integrative framework. *Journal of Environmental Psychology, 15*(3), 169–182. https://doi.org/10.1016/0272-4944(95)90001-2

Kearney, A. R. (2006). Residential development patterns and neighborhood satisfaction. *Environment and Behavior, 38*(1), 112–139. https://doi.org/10.1177/0013916505277607

Kellert, S., & Wilson, E. (1993). *The biophilia hypothesis*. Island Press.

Kemperman, A., & Timmermans, H. (2014). Green spaces in the direct living environment and social contacts of the aging population. *Landscape and Urban Planning, 129*, 44–54. https://doi.org/10.1016/j.landurbplan.2014.05.003

Kim, G., & Miller, P. A. (2019). The impact of green infrastructure on human health and well-being: The example of the Huckleberry Trail and the Heritage Community Park and natural area in Blacksburg, Virginia. *Sustainable Cities and Society, 48*, 101562. https://doi.org/10.1016/j.scs.2019.101562

Kim, J., & Kaplan, R. (2004). Physical and psychological factors in sense of community: New urbanist Kentlands and nearby Orchard Village. *Environment and Behavior*, *36*(3), 313–340. https://doi.org/10.1177/0013916503260236

Kley, S., & Dovbischuk, T. (2021). How a lack of green in the residential environment lowers the life satisfaction of city dwellers and increases their willingness to relocate. *Sustainability*, *13*(7), 3984. https://doi.org/10.3390/su13073984

Kley, S., & Dovbischuk, T. (2024). The equigenic potential of green window views for city dwellers' well-being. *Sustainable Cities and Society*, *108*, 105511. https://doi.org/10.1016/j.scs.2024.105511

Korpela, K. M., Hartig, T., Kaiser, F. G., & Fuhrer, U. (2001). Restorative experience and self-regulation in favorite places. *Environment and Behavior*, *33*(4), 572–589. https://doi.org/10.1177/00139160121973133

Krekel, C., Kolbe, J., & Wüstemann, H. (2016). The greener, the happier? The effect of urban land use on residential well-being. *Ecological Economics*, *121*, 117–127. https://doi.org/10.1016/j.ecolecon.2015.11.005

Kweon, B.-S., Ellis, C., Leiva, P., & Rogers, G. (2010). Landscape components, land use, and neighborhood satisfaction. *Environment and Planning B: Planning and Design*, *37*, 500–517. https://doi.org/10.1068/b35059

Lachowycz, K., Jones, A. P., Page, A. S., Wheeler, B. W., & Cooper, A. R. (2012). What can global positioning systems tell us about the contribution of different types of urban greenspace to children's physical activity? *Health & Place*, *18*(3), 586–594. https://doi.org/10.1016/j.healthplace.2012.01.006

Lee, S. M., Conway, T. L., Frank, L. D., Saelens, B. E., Cain, K. L., & Sallis, J. F. (2016). The relation of perceived and objective environment attributes to neighborhood satisfaction. *Environment and Behavior*, *49*(2), 136–160. https://doi.org/10.1177/0013916515623823

Lindal, P. J., & Hartig, T. (2015). Effects of urban street vegetation on judgments of restoration likelihood. *Urban Forestry & Urban Greening*, *14*(2), 200–209. https://doi.org/10.1016/j.ufug.2015.02.001

Lovasi, G. S., Schwartz-Soicher, O., Quinn, J. W., Berger, D. K., Neckerman, K. M., Jaslow, R., Lee, K. K., & Rundle, A. (2013). Neighborhood safety and green space as predictors of obesity among preschool children from low-income families in New York city. *Preventive Medicine*, *57*(3), 189–193. https://doi.org/10.1016/j.ypmed.2013.05.012

Ma, B., Zhou, T. T., Lei, S., Wen, Y. L., & Htun, T. T. (2019). Effects of urban green spaces on residents' well-being. *Environment Development and Sustainability*, *21*(6), 2793–2809. https://doi.org/10.1007/s10668-018-0161-8

Maas, J., van Dillen, S. M. E., Verheij, R. A., & Groenewegen, P. P. (2009). Social contacts as a possible mechanism behind the relation between green space and health. *Health & Place*, *15*(2), 586–595. https://doi.org/10.1016/j.healthplace.2008.09.006

MacKerron, G., & Mourato, S. (2013). Happiness is greater in natural environments. *Global Environmental Change*, *23*(5), 992–1000. https://doi.org/10.1016/j.gloenvcha.2013.03.010

Mak, B. K. L., & Jim, C. Y. (2019). Linking park users' socio-demographic characteristics and visit-related preferences to improve urban parks. *Cities*, *92*, 97–111. https://doi.org/10.1016/j.cities.2019.03.008

Martin, L., White, M. P., Hunt, A., Richardson, M., Pahl, S., & Burt, J. (2020). Nature contact, nature connectedness and associations with health, wellbeing and pro-environmental behaviours. *Journal of Environmental Psychology*, *68*, 101389. https://doi.org/10.1016/j.jenvp.2020.101389

Mayer, F. S., McPherson Franz, C., & Bruehlman-Senecal, E. (2009). Why is nature beneficial? The role of connectedness to nature. *Environment and Behavior*, *41*(5), 607–643. https://doi.org/10.1177/0013916508319745

Mohai, P., & Saha, R. (2015). Which came first, people or pollution? A review of theory and evidence from longitudinal environmental justice studies. *Environmental Research Letters*, *10*(12), 125011. https://doi.org/10.1088/1748-9326/10/12/125011

Nisbet, E. K., Zelenski, J. M., & Murphy, S. A. (2009). The nature relatedness scale. *Environment and Behavior*, *41*(5), 715–740. https://doi.org/10.1177/0013916508318748

Park, G., & Evans, G. W. (2016). Environmental stressors, urban design and planning: Implications for human behaviour and health. *Journal of Urban Design*, *21*(4), 453–470. https://doi.org/10.1080/13574809.2016.1194189

Pinto, L., Ferreira, C. S. S., & Pereira, P. (2021). Environmental and socioeconomic factors influencing the use of urban green spaces in Coimbra (Portugal). *Science of the Total Environment*, *792*, 148293. https://doi.org/10.1016/j.scitotenv.2021.148293

Preisendörfer, P., Liebe, U., Bruderer Enzler, H., & Diekmann, A. (2022). Annoyance due to residential road traffic and aircraft noise: Empirical evidence from two European cities. *Environmental Research*, *206*, 112269. https://doi.org/10.1016/j.envres.2021.112269

Refisch, M., Kurz, K., & Hartmann, J. (2024). Urban green space usage and life satisfaction during the COVID-19 pandemic. *Applied Research in Quality of Life*. https://doi.org/10.1007/s11482-024-10279-z

Rigolon, A., Browning, M. H. E. M., McAnirlin, O., & Yoon, H. (2021). Green space and health equity: A systematic review on the potential of green space to reduce health disparities. *International Journal of Environmental Research and Public Health*, *18*(5), 2563. https://doi.org/10.3390/ijerph18052563

Säumel, I., Hogrefe, J., Battisti, L., Wachtel, T., & Larcher, F. (2021). The healthy green living room at one's doorstep? Use and perception of residential greenery in Berlin, Germany. *Urban Forestry & Urban Greening*, *58*, 126949. https://doi.org/10.1016/j.ufug.2020.126949

Seresinhe, C. I., Preis, T., Mackerron, G., & Moat, H. S. (2019). Happiness is greater in more scenic locations. *Scientific Reports*, *9*(1). https://doi.org/10.1038/s41598-019-40854-6

Stigsdotter, U. K., Ekholm, O., Schipperijn, J., Toftager, M., Kamper-Jorgensen, F., & Randrup, T. B. (2010). Health promoting outdoor environments – associations between green space, and health, health-related quality of life and stress based on a Danish national representative survey. *Scandinavian Journal of Public Health*, *38*(4), 411–417. https://doi.org/10.1177/1403494810367468

Taylor, A. F., & Kuo, F. E. (2009). Children with attention deficits concentrate better after walk in the park. *Journal of Attention Disorders*, *12*(5), 402–409. https://doi.org/10.1177/1087054708323000

Tinsley, H. E., Tinsley, D. J., & Croskeys, C. E. (2002). Park usage, social milieu, and psychosocial benefits of park use reported by older urban park users from four ethnic groups. *Leisure Sciences*, *24*(2), 199–218. https://doi.org/10.1080/01490400252900158

Ulrich, R. (1984). View through a window may influence recovery from surgery. *Science*, *224*, 420–421. https://doi.org/10.1126/science.6143402

Ulrich, R., Simons, R., Losito, B., Fiorito, E., Miles, M., & Zelson, M. (1991). Stress recovery during exposure to natural and urban environments. *Journal of Environmental Psychology*, *11*, 201–230. https://doi.org/10.1016/S0272-4944(05)80184-7

van den Berg, A. E., Maas, J., Verheij, R. A., & Groenewegen, P. P. (2010). Green space as a buffer between stressful life events and health. *Social Science & Medicine*, *70*(8), 1203–1210. https://doi.org/10.1016/j.socscimed.2010.01.002

Van Herzele, A., & De Vries, S. (2012). Linking green space to health: A comparative study of two urban neighbourhoods in Ghent, Belgium. *Population and Environment*, *34*(2), 171–193. https://doi.org/10.1007/s11111-011-0153-1

Wang, R., Feng, Z., & Pearce, J. (2022). Neighbourhood greenspace quantity, quality and socioeconomic inequalities in mental health. *Cities*, *129*. https://doi.org/10.1016/j.cities.2022.103815

Wei, D., Lu, Y., Wu, X., Ho, H. C., Wu, W., Song, J., & Wang, Y. (2023). Greenspace exposure may increase life expectancy of elderly adults, especially for those with low socioeconomic status. *Health & Place*, *84*, 103142. https://doi.org/10.1016/j.healthplace.2023.103142

White, M. P., Alcock, I., Wheeler, B. W., & Depledge, M. H. (2013). Would you be happier living in a greener urban area? A fixed-effects analysis of panel data. *Psychological Science*, *24*(6), 920–928. https://doi.org/10.1177/0956797612464659

Wolch, J., Wilson, J. P., & Fehrenbach, J. (2005). Parks and park funding in Los Angeles: An equity-mapping analysis. *Urban Geography*, *26*(1), 4–35. https://doi.org/10.2747/0272-3638.26.1.4

Wolch, J. R., Byrne, J., & Newell, J. P. (2014). Urban green space, public health, and environmental justice: The challenge of making cities 'just green enough'. *Landscape and Urban Planning*, *125*, 234–244. https://doi.org/10.1016/j.landurbplan.2014.01.017

World Health Organization. (2017). *Urban green spaces*. Author.

Wu, W., Dong, G., Sun, Y., & Yun, Y. (2020). Contextualized effects of park access and usage on residential satisfaction: A spatial approach. *Land Use Policy*, *94*. https://doi.org/10.1016/j.landusepol.2020.104532

Zhang, Y., van den Berg, A. E., Van Dijk, T., & Weitkamp, G. (2017). Quality over quantity: Contribution of urban green space to neighborhood satisfaction. *International Journal of Environmental Research and Public Health*, *14*(5), 535. https://doi.org/10.3390/ijerph14050535

Zhao, Y., van den Berg, P. E. W., Ossokina, I. V., & Arentze, T. A. (2024). How do urban parks, neighborhood open spaces, and private gardens relate to individuals' subjective well-being: Results of a structural equation model. *Sustainable Cities and Society*, *101*, 105094. https://doi.org/10.1016/j.scs.2023.105094

2 Research design

The current study (Kley & Dovbischuk, 2023) was designed as a two-wave study in two major German cities, Cologne and Hamburg. It builds primarily on the work of Kley (2009, 2011), who focused on explaining migration decisions and emphasised the importance of the decision-making process prior to migration implementation. Her study, based on a multi-wave telephone survey in Magdeburg and Freiburg, Germany, focused on two key aspects. First, it examined the stages of the migration decision-making process, including considering and planning migration, and the subsequent realisation of migration intentions. Second, the study analysed the differences among the individual life course phases, including the early adulthood phase, the family phase, and the consolidation phase.

Some elements of this study have parallels with the reference work by Kley (2009, 2011), especially in relation to relocation processes. However, the core focus of the current study in Hamburg and Cologne differs considerably, as it aims to understand the role of green spaces in influencing both quality of life and relocation processes in urban environments. Originally focusing on the relevance of green spaces for residential mobility within cities, the selection of study locations required areas with a large spatial extent and a high proportion of annual inner-city moves. Therefore, only the four largest German cities (see Table 2.1) were considered for further analysis. The study locations of Cologne and Hamburg were selected on the basis of strict criteria, including population size, frequency of inner-city relocations, proportion of green space, segregation index, and the distance required for a middle-income family to afford adequate housing.

There is no official method for determining the proportion of green space at city level. However, as the subjective assessment of the human eye could correspond well with the visual perception of green areas on satellite imagery, the evaluation of satellite imagery for the classification of green areas in Germany (Tröger et al., 2016) is used as a reference. This classification focuses on the evaluation of actual green areas and is not based on official land use information. Hamburg stands out as the German city with the highest proportion of green areas, at 71%. Cologne, on the other hand, has a comparatively low

DOI: 10.4324/9781003546146-3

Table 2.1 Relevant key figures for the four largest German cities

	Number of inhabitants (in thousands)	*Inner-city relocations*	*Proportion of green spaces*[1]	*Segregation index*[2]	*Distance needed for a middle-income family to afford adequate housing*[3]
Berlin	3 851[4]	4.4%	59.0% (530 km^2)	31.3	8 km
Cologne	1 085[5]	6.7%	58.4% (240 km^2)	31.9	13 km
Hamburg	1 854[6]	6.3%	71.4% (540 km^2)	25.9	27 km
Munich	1 562[7]	7.3%	49.9% (160 km^2)	21.5	40 km

Notes

1 Area covered with vegetation, based on satellite images (Tröger et al., 2016).

2 Calculated on the basis of recipients of social welfare benefits in 2014 (Helbig & Jähnen, 2018).

3 Kilometres represent the linear distance between the city centre and the area in which middle-income family households would find suitable and affordable housing. The value range is between 1 and 50, as housing that is more than 50 kilometres from the city centre is not assessed. A higher value indicates a lower supply of family-friendly and affordable housing (Heyn et al., 2013).

4 The reference date for calculating the number of inhabitants and the proportion of inner-city relocations is 31 December 2022 (Amt für Statistik Berlin-Brandenburg, 2023, 2024).

5 Reference date: 31 December 2017 (Stadt Köln – Amt für Stadtentwicklung und Statistik, 2019).

6 Reference date: 31 December 2022 (Statistisches Amt für Hamburg und Schleswig-Holstein, 2023).

7 Reference date: 31 December 2021 (Statistisches Amt der Landeshauptstadt München, 2021).

proportion of green space (58%). The difference in the proportion of green space between these two selected cities makes it possible, on the one hand, to examine whether the role of green space changes as the environment becomes greener. On the other hand, it allows an assessment of whether inequalities in well-being across life course phases or social classes can be minimised with a higher proportion of green space (as has been done in previous research, e.g. Kley & Dovbischuk, 2024).

The segregation index quantifies the extent of socio-economic disparities between affluent and less affluent neighbourhoods within a city. Cities such as Berlin with a segregation index of 31.3 and Cologne with 31.9 are characterised by high levels of segregation. In contrast, Munich (21.5) and Hamburg (25.9) have comparatively lower segregation indices (Helbig & Jähnen, 2018). A comparison of megacities with different segregation indices could provide deeper insights into spatial inequalities in wealth distribution. For this reason, Cologne and Hamburg again meet the selection criteria. Although Munich also has a low level of segregation, it is less suitable for the analysis due to its very high housing market prices, which are reflected in the distance index developed by the Bertelsmann Foundation (Heyn et al., 2013). This index indicates the distance from the city centre within which middle-income family households can find suitable and affordable housing. In Munich, middle-income families have to move over a considerable distance of 40 kilometres from the city centre to find suitable housing. In Hamburg, this distance is reduced to 27 kilometres, and in Cologne to 13 kilometres, allowing both a direct comparison between Hamburg and Cologne, and the pooling of data from two cities for analysis. When pooling the data, as in this work, the affiliation to the city is controlled for throughout the models.

Field study information

The sample of private households in Cologne and Hamburg was randomly drawn using the Gabler–Häder method (Häder & Sand, 2019). The parent population, which was estimated at 56,000 landline numbers based on the required number of contact attempts in the reference study (Kley, 2009), was formed using the Random Digit Dialing (RDD) method. As it is not possible to restrict the mobile phone numbers spatially to the cities of Hamburg and Cologne, the sample selection was limited to a landline sample. In the RDD method, the number of landline telephone numbers required for the calculated parent population was generated using a random sequence of digits with predefined area codes for Hamburg (040) and Cologne (0220). The RDD method covers all households with a telephone connection, regardless of provider or telephone directory listing.[1]

In order to avoid clustering effects that could lead to the grouping of social class characteristics and influence the social status of the final sample, only one person from each household was randomly selected to participate in the study. To ensure random selection at the household level, the last birthday method was used, that is, the person in the household with the most recent birthday was selected. This pseudo-probabilistic method is approximately equivalent to a random selection of individuals in the household (see Gaziano, 2005). The sampling design for drawing a landline sample already carries the risk of distortions in the final sample due to different selection probabilities in households of different sizes. These distortions are corrected by the household weight, which is defined as the multiplicative inverse of the reduced household size (i.e. 1/number of target individuals in the household). The household weight is used for all analyses in this work.

The main survey of the first wave of the study, which included 1,909 participants, took place between 9 September 2020 and 10 February 2021. During this period, computer-assisted telephone interviews (CATI) were conducted in the urban areas of Hamburg and Cologne. The questionnaire for the first wave began with a screening section to determine whether the person selected in the household using the last birthday method could be included in the study sample. Two criteria were applied: first, individuals had to be at least 18 years old; and second, they had to have lived in their current dwelling for at least one year. The latter criterion of length of residence was applied uniformly to all respondents due to daily adjustments, despite the extension of the field period to six months.

In addition to these criteria, the screening questionnaire was used to determine whether the target person belonged to the group of respondents who were considering relocation,[2] as those who were considering relocation were intentionally oversampled. In addition, two slightly different versions of the subsequent questionnaires were used for individuals with and without relocation considerations. The sample size for Cologne comprised 950 respondents, of whom 450 were considering relocation and 500 were not. For Hamburg, the sample size was 959 respondents, of whom 459 were considering relocation and 500 were not.

As mentioned earlier, respondents considering relocation were intentionally included in the sample at a higher rate than their distribution in the population. The actual distribution of those considering relocation in the population is not known. Therefore, the weighting was calculated on the following basis: the ratio of completed interviews on the day the quota of persons not considering relocation (50%) was reached should reflect the actual distribution of persons considering relocation in the population. Table 2.2 shows the ratio of these two groups of respondents (with vs. without relocation considerations) on the days when the quotas were reached – 26 October 2020 in Hamburg and 28 November 2020 in Cologne. As the difference between the two cities is minimal (77% in Cologne vs. 79% in Hamburg not considering relocation), there is no reason why the datasets of the two cities should not be pooled. The oversampling weighting was determined on the basis of this ratio and, together with the household weighting mentioned earlier, is consistently applied to the results presented in this work.

Follow-up survey

First of all, it is important to clarify that only data from the first wave are considered in this work. Therefore, the information on the follow-up survey is briefly outlined below without going into detail. As the main survey in the first wave described earlier served as the starting point for a two-wave longitudinal study, participants' willingness to be interviewed again was assessed at the first interview. Willingness fluctuated over time, ranging from 54% in early October 2020 to 92% in mid-November 2020, with an average willingness to

Table 2.2 Calculation of the design weighting based on the distribution of respondents considering and not considering relocation in the population and in the sample

	Do not consider relocation	*Consider relocation*	*Total*
Cologne			
Number of respondents in parent population	500	147	647
(Reference date: 28 November 2020)			
Percentage in parent population	77.3%	22.7%	100%
Adjusted sample	500	450	950
Rounded weighting	1.468	0.480	–
Hamburg			
Number of respondents in parent population	500	133	633
(Reference date: 26 October 2020)			
Percentage in parent population	79.0%	21.0%	100%
Adjusted sample	500	459	959
Rounded weighting	1.515	0.439	–

participate in the follow-up survey of 78%. Brief interviews were conducted between surveys to maintain participant engagement and motivation. Additionally, two online strategies were developed. First, a project website was set up to provide all relevant information on the progress of the study.[3] Participants were invited to visit this website at the end of their interviews. Second, a project Twitter account was set up to facilitate direct communication.[4] Throughout the project, flyers explaining the research questions, methods, and data handling were designed and distributed to participants both directly and through the online platforms.

As at least half of the respondents were individuals who were considering relocation, it was important to keep them in the sample in case they moved. Participants were asked to provide new contact details in the event of a relocation. In addition, short interviews were conducted to keep participants motivated. If a relocation had already taken place at the time of the short interview, the follow-up questionnaire was used immediately.

The second wave was conducted approximately 12 months after the first wave. A mixed mode approach was used for those who had not moved at the time of the short interviews. Participants could choose between a telephone interview (CATI) and a computer-assisted web interview (CAWI). A total of 977 interviews were conducted in the second wave of the study, representing a participation rate of 51%. The data from the second wave are not included in the current work, as only the data from the first wave are used for the following analyses.

Demographic characteristics in the sample and in the official statistics

A comparison of the sample with the official statistics for the cities of Hamburg and Cologne shows that in both cities, women are slightly overrepresented in the sample, and men are somewhat underrepresented (see Table 2.3). On average, respondents in Hamburg and Cologne are older than the resident population, with those aged 35–44 and those aged 75 and over reflecting the proportion of the overall population in the cities. Respondents are also more likely to be married and less likely to be single. Compared with official statistics, respondents with A-level qualifications are overrepresented, while those

Table 2.3 Distribution of demographic characteristics in the sample and in the official statistics in Hamburg (*N* = 930) and Cologne (*N* = 910), estimates design weighted

	Hamburg sample	*Official statistics*[1]	*Cologne sample*	*Official statistics*[2]	*Total sample*
Female	55.4%	51.0%	58.1%	51.1%	56.7%
Male	44.6%	49.0%	41.9%	48.9%	43.3%
Age					
18–24	3.8%	8.0%	7.2%	8.4%	5.4%
25–29	2.8%	8.0%	3.0%	8.5%	2.9%
30–34	3.7%	8.4%	3.9%	8.1%	3.8%
35–39	8.3%	7.7%	7.0%	7.6%	7.7%
40–44	6.8%	6.7%	8.1%	6.8%	7.5%
45–54	23.6%	14.6%	24.0%	15.3%	23.8%
55–59	12.2%	6.6%	12.3%	6.5%	12.3%
60–64	10.2%	5.1%	12.3%	5.2%	11.3%
65–74	17.8%	8.4%	14.3%	8.3%	16.1%
75 years or older	10.7%	9.9%	7.8%	9.2%	9.3%
Single	20.9%	52.0%	25.4%	48.4%	23.1%
Married	63.3%	34.7%	61.4%	37.1%	62.3%
Divorced	7.4%	8.1%	7.5%	7.7%	7.4%
Widowed	8.5%	5.2%	5.8%	5.3%	7.2%
Highest school degree					
Up to some secondary school	12.9%	25.0%	12.2%	16.0%	12.5%
Secondary school	30.7%	25.1%	25.0%	25.0%	27.9%
Advanced technical college	9.9%	8.3%	8.0%	55.0%	9.0%
A-levels	46.5%	33.3%	54.8%		50.6%
Employed, full time	46.2%	37.8%	47.8%	38.6%	47.0%
Employed, part time	15.3%	14.5%	15.1%	15.1%	15.2%
With migration background	24.7%	35.5%	26.7%	38.2%	25.7%
One-person household	21.1%	54.5%	22.0%	50.4%	21.6%

(*Continued*)

Table 2.3 (Continued)

	Hamburg sample	*Official statistics*[1]	*Cologne sample*	*Official statistics*[2]	*Total sample*
Household with child(ren)	35.1%	17.8%	33.8%	18.5%	34.5%
Persons per household	2.45	1.84	2.45	1.88	2.45

Notes

1 Reference date for gender and age data, data on marital status, migration background, and information on the composition of persons in the household in Hamburg: 31 December 2018 (Statistisches Amt für Hamburg und Schleswig-Holstein, 2020). Reference date for data on school degrees (for people aged 15 and over) in Hamburg: 9 May 2011 (Statistisches Amt für Hamburg und Schleswig-Holstein, 2016). Reference date for information on employment status in Hamburg: 30 June 2017 (Statistisches Amt für Hamburg und Schleswig-Holstein, 2018).

2 Reference date for information on gender and age, marital status, migration background, and the composition of persons in the household in Cologne: 31 December 2017. The information on school degrees is rounded and comes from the representative population survey 'Living in Cologne' from 2016, N = ca. 14,400 (Stadt Köln – Amt für Stadtentwicklung und Statistik, 2019). Reference date for information on employment status in Cologne: 30 June 2017 (Kölner Statistische Nachrichten, 2021).

with the highest level of education up to some secondary education are underrepresented. Full-time workers are somewhat overrepresented in the sample, while part-time workers are about the same as in the population. As expected, individuals with a migration background are underrepresented in both cities, probably due to the fact that the survey was conducted in German. In terms of household composition, respondents are less likely to live in single-person households, resulting in a higher average number of household members. In addition, households with child(ren) are slightly overrepresented in the sample.

Overall, the comparison with official sociodemographic data shows that men, younger respondents, households without children, and single-person households are underrepresented. People with a lower level of education and respondents with a migration background are also underrepresented. However, these discrepancies are common in population surveys and correspond to well-established patterns of participation behaviour (for further discussion, cf. Häder & Sand, 2019, p. 61f; Koch, 1998; Schneekloth & Leven, 2003). Due to the complex random sampling methodology with a high number of contact attempts,[5] the quality of the data collected is considered to be high.

Shaping a robust research design

The random selection of landline numbers in Cologne and Hamburg was carried out using the RDD method (Häder & Sand, 2019). This method considers all households with a telephone connection, regardless of the provider or telephone directory listing. This approach has become established as a selection frame in Germany and is updated twice a year. The analysis focused exclusively on households that could be reached via the landline network, as the survey locations were limited to the urban areas of Cologne and Hamburg, and it was not possible to restrict the mobile phone numbers to these urban areas. Furthermore, the exact percentage of households without a landline is not known, but estimates based on Hamburg data from 2016 suggest that it was only 12.5% (Bock & Schnapp, 2016). Overall, the lack of a landline should not be systematically correlated with the relationships analysed in this study (nature use and nature satisfaction). Therefore, possible biases due to this sampling method, if any, are considered to be minimal.

Up to 13 contact attempts were then made to reach the telephone numbers generated by the RDD approach in order to improve data quality. Seventy-three percent of interviews were successfully completed within a maximum of three contact attempts (33% on the first and 26% on the second attempt). The number of contact attempts required to complete an interview decreased significantly after the third contact attempt, which is associated with higher data quality (see, e.g. Fricker & Tourangeau, 2010; Olson, 2013).

The minimum response rate for the survey was 7.3%. According to the standard definitions of AAPOR (2016), which distinguish among different response rates, the minimum response rate is calculated by dividing the number of completed interviews by the sum of completed and partial interviews, non-interviews, and cases with unknown eligibility. It is not uncommon for telephone surveys to have low response rates. In the United States, the average landline response rate was 9.3% in 2015 (AAPOR, 2018), while the Gallup Poll Social Series achieved a response rate of 7% in 2017 (Marken, 2018). A lower response rate may affect the accuracy of the results but does not make the data less reliable (Meterko et al., 2015), especially if the survey is conducted using a strict probability sampling method.

While the current sample has certain limitations, such as a relatively low response rate, underrepresentation of younger individuals, or overrepresentation of those with higher levels of education, this type of probability sampling is notably less prone to error compared to commonly used non-probability sampling methods, such as quota samples, convenience samples, or access panels, when addressing similar research questions on the relevance of green space to well-being outcomes (e.g. Bertram & Rehdanz, 2015; Chiesura, 2004; Coppel & Wüstemann, 2017; Grima et al., 2020; Honold et al., 2016; Irvine et al., 2013; Kaplan, 2001; Kearney, 2006; Kim & Miller, 2019; Kim & Kaplan, 2004; Korpela et al., 2001; MacKerron & Mourato, 2013; Pinto et al., 2021; Puhakka et al., 2018; Tinsley et al., 2002; White et al., 2010; Zhao et al., 2024). For instance, research in the United States by Yeager et al. (2011) found that probability sampling surveys were consistently more accurate than non-probability sampling surveys for sociodemographic variables, housing variables, and health measures, even when the latter used post-stratification weighting, which is often completely neglected. Non-probability sampling methods may have economic advantages, but there are inevitable quality trade-offs. These trade-offs remain even when the probability samples have relatively low response rates (Cornesse et al., 2020; Kohler & Post, 2023), as in the case of the present study.

Data processing and analysis

For some survey questions, respondents were given the opportunity to provide additional information if none of the given options applied. Approximately 7,000 responses of this type were manually coded in preparing the database for analysis. MAXQDA 2020 was used for this coding process. The subsequent statistical analyses were carried out using Stata 18. Analyses based on spatial information were carried out using QGIS 3.26.1.

Notes

1 The sampling framework developed by GESIS based on the Gabler–Häder design (Häder & Sand, 2019) is updated twice a year (see www.gesis.org/en/services/planning-studies-and-collecting-data/sampling).
2 The question was: 'Have you recently thought about moving out of your flat or house to live somewhere else?' The term 'recently' referred to the last three months. Clarification on this time reference was provided on request.
3 The project website can be found at www.wiso.uni-hamburg.de/wohnstudie (in German or English).
4 The project's Twitter profile can be found at https://twitter.com/Wohnstudie_UHH (maintained until September 2023).
5 Up to 13 contact attempts were made, with an average of 2.76 contact attempts to complete the full interview. Although up to 13 contact attempts were made, the number decreases significantly after three contact attempts. A lower number of contact attempts correlates with higher data quality (see, e.g. Fricker & Tourangeau, 2010; Olson, 2013).

References

AAPOR. (2016). *Standard definitions: Final dispositions of case codes and outcome rates for surveys* (9th ed.). A. A. F. P. O. Research.
AAPOR. (2018). *The future of U.S. general population telephone survey research.* AAPOR Report. American Association for Public Opinion Research.
Amt für Statistik Berlin-Brandenburg. (2023). *Statistischer bericht, wanderungen im land Berlin 2022*. Report No. AIII2-j/22. https://download.statistik-berlin-brandenburg.de/f120071ff74761c9/5e3bf960d3b0/SB_A03-02-00_2022j01_BE.pdf

Amt für Statistik Berlin-Brandenburg. (2024). *Statistischer bericht, einwohnerregisterstatistik Berlin 31 Dezember 2023*. Report No. AI5-hj2/23. https://download.statistik-berlin-brandenburg.de/33c9036f104cc704/506649c17098/SB_A01-05-00_2023h02_BE.pdf

Bertram, C., & Rehdanz, K. (2015). The role of urban green space for human well-being. *Ecological Economics*, *120*, 139–152. https://doi.org/10.1016/j.ecolecon.2015.10.013

Bock, O., & Schnapp, K.-U. (2016). *Hamburg-BUS: Feldbericht 2016*. www.wiso.uni-hamburg.de/forschung/archiv/hhbus-files/feldbericht2016.pdf

Chiesura, A. (2004). The role of urban parks for the sustainable city. *Landscape and Urban Planning*, *68*(1), 129–138. https://doi.org/10.1016/j.landurbplan.2003.08.003

Coppel, G., & Wüstemann, H. (2017). The impact of urban green space on health in Berlin, Germany: Empirical findings and implications for urban planning. *Landscape and Urban Planning*, *167*, 410–418. https://doi.org/10.1016/j.landurbplan.2017.06.015

Cornesse, C., Blom, A. G., Dutwin, D., Krosnick, J. A., De Leeuw, E. D., Legleye, S., Pasek, J., Pennay, D., Phillips, B., Sakshaug, J. W., Struminskaya, B., & Wenz, A. (2020). A review of conceptual approaches and empirical evidence on probability and nonprobability sample survey research. *Journal of Survey Statistics and Methodology*, *8*(1), 4–36. https://doi.org/10.1093/jssam/smz041

Fricker, S., & Tourangeau, R. (2010). Examining the relationship between nonresponse propensity and data quality in two national household surveys. *Public Opinion Quarterly*, *74*(5), 934–955. https://doi.org/10.1093/poq/nfq064

Gaziano, C. (2005). Comparative analysis of within-household respondent selection techniques. *Public Opinion Quarterly*, *69*(1), 124–157. https://doi.org/10.1093/poq/nfi006

Grima, N., Corcoran, W., Hill-James, C., Langton, B., Sommer, H., & Fisher, B. (2020). The importance of urban natural areas and urban ecosystem services during the COVID-19 pandemic. *PLoS One*, *15*(12), e0243344. https://doi.org/10.1371/journal.pone.0243344

Häder, S., & Sand, M. (2019). Telefonstichproben. In S. Häder, M. Häder, & P. Schmich (Eds.), *Telefonumfragen in Deutschland* (pp. 45–80). Springer VS.

Helbig, M., & Jähnen, S. (2018). Wie brüchig ist die soziale Architektur unserer Städte? *Trends und Analysen der Segregation in 74 deutschen Städten* (No. P 2018-001). WZB Discussion Paper

Heyn, T., Braun, R., Grade, J., Heyn, T., Braun, R., & Grade, J. (2013). *Wohnungsangebot für arme Familien in Großstädten*. Bertelsmann-Stiftung.

Honold, J., Lakes, T., Beyer, R., & van der Meer, E. (2016). Restoration in urban spaces: Nature views from home, greenways, and public parks. *Environment and Behavior*, *48*(6), 796–825. https://doi.org/10.1177/0013916514568555

Irvine, K. N., Warber, S. L., Devine-Wright, P., & Gaston, K. J. (2013). Understanding urban green space as a health resource: A qualitative comparison of visit motivation and derived effects among park users in Sheffield, UK. *International Journal of Environmental Research and Public Health*, *10*(1), 417–442. https://doi.org/10.3390/ijerph10010417

Kaplan, R. (2001). The nature of the view from home. *Environment and Behavior*, *33*(4), 507–542. https://doi.org/10.1177/00139160121973115

Kearney, A. R. (2006). Residential development patterns and neighborhood satisfaction. *Environment and Behavior*, *38*(1), 112–139. https://doi.org/10.1177/0013916505277607

Kim, G., & Miller, P. A. (2019). The impact of green infrastructure on human health and well-being: The example of the Huckleberry Trail and the Heritage Community Park and natural area in Blacksburg, Virginia. *Sustainable Cities and Society*, *48*, 101562. https://doi.org/10.1016/j.scs.2019.101562

Kim, J., & Kaplan, R. (2004). Physical and psychological factors in sense of community: New urbanist Kentlands and nearby Orchard Village. *Environment and Behavior*, *36*(3), 313–340. https://doi.org/10.1177/0013916503260236

Kley, S. (2009). *Migration im Lebensverlauf. Der Einfluss von Lebensbedingungen und Lebenslaufereignissen auf den Wohnortwechsel*. VS Verlag für Sozialwissenschaften.

Kley, S. (2011). Explaining the stages of migration within a life-course framework. *European Sociological Review*, *27*(4), 469–486. https://doi.org/10.1093/esr/jcq020

Kley, S., & Dovbischuk, T. (2023). Soziale Selektivität von Wohnstandortentscheidungen im Hinblick auf Grünräume und ihre Auswirkungen auf die Lebensqualität (Datenfile Version 1.0.0.). GESIS.

Kley, S., & Dovbischuk, T. (2024). The equigenic potential of green window views for city dwellers' well-being. *Sustainable Cities and Society*, *108*, 105511. https://doi.org/10.1016/j.scs.2024.105511

Koch, A. (1998). Wenn "mehr" nicht gleichbedeutend mit "besser" ist: Ausschöpfungsquoten und Stichprobenverzerrungen in allgemeinen Bevölkerungsumfragen. *Zuma Nachrichten*, *22*(42), 66–90.

Kohler, U., & Post, J. C. (2023). Welcher Zweck heiligt die Mittel. Bemerkungen zur Repräsentativitätsdebatte in der Meinungsforschung. *Zeitschrift für Soziologie*, *52*(1), 67–88. https://doi.org/10.1515/zfsoz-2023-2001

Kölner Statistische Nachrichten. (2021). *Arbeitsmarkt Köln. Corona-Krise: Rückblick 2020, bisherige Entwicklung und Ausblick 2021*. www.stadt-koeln.de/mediaasset/content/pdf15/statistik-wirtschaft-und-arbeitsmarkt/arbeitsmarkt_k%C3%B6ln_corona-krise_r%C3%BCckblick_2020.pdf

Korpela, K. M., Hartig, T., Kaiser, F. G., & Fuhrer, U. (2001). Restorative experience and self-regulation in favorite places. *Environment and Behavior*, *33*(4), 572–589. https://doi.org/10.1177/00139160121973133

MacKerron, G., & Mourato, S. (2013). Happiness is greater in natural environments. *Global Environmental Change*, *23*(5), 992–1000. https://doi.org/10.1016/j.gloenvcha.2013.03.010

Marken, S. (2018). *Still listening: The state of telephone surveys*. Gallup.

Meterko, M., Restuccia, J. D., Stolzmann, K., Mohr, D., Brennan, C., Glasgow, J., & Kaboli, P. (2015). Response rates, nonresponse bias, and data quality: Results from a national survey of senior healthcare leaders. *Public Opinion Quarterly*, *79*(1), 130–144. https://doi.org/10.1093/poq/nfu052

Olson, K. (2013). Do non-response follow-ups improve or reduce data quality?: A review of the existing literature. *Journal of the Royal Statistical Society Series A: Statistics in Society*, *176*(1), 129–145. https://doi.org/10.1111/j.1467-985X.2012.01042.x

Pinto, L., Ferreira, C. S. S., & Pereira, P. (2021). Environmental and socioeconomic factors influencing the use of urban green spaces in Coimbra (Portugal). *Science of the Total Environment*, *792*, 148293. https://doi.org/10.1016/j.scitotenv.2021.148293

Puhakka, S., Pyky, R., Lankila, T., Kangas, M., Rusanen, J., Ikäheimo, T. M., Koivumaa-Honkanen, H., & Korpelainen, R. (2018). Physical activity, residential environment, and nature relatedness in young men – A population-based MOPO study. *International Journal of Environmental Research and Public Health*, *15*(10), 2322. https://doi.org/10.3390/ijerph15102322

Schneekloth, U., & Leven, I. (2003). Woran bemisst sich eine "gute" allgemeine Bevölkerungsumfrage? Analysen zu Ausmaß, Bedeutung und zu den Hintergründen von Nonresponse in zufallsbasierten stichprobenerhebungen am Beispiel des ALLBUS. *Zuma Nachrichten*, *27*(53), 16–57.

Stadt Köln – Amt für Stadtentwicklung und Statistik. (2019). *Statistisches Jahrbuch Köln 2018*. www.stadt-koeln.de/mediaasset/content/pdf15/15_statistisches_jahrbuch_2018_bfrei.pdf

Statistisches Amt der Landeshauptstadt München. (2021). *Statistisches Taschenbuch 2021. München und seine Stadtbezirke*. https://stadt.muenchen.de/dam/jcr:cc9cc6c7-cfd6-4d9a-8f33-bed0dbec974a/LHM_Stat.pdf

Statistisches Amt für Hamburg und Schleswig-Holstein. (2016). *Metropolregion Hamburg. Endgültige Ergebnisse des Zensus vom 9. Mai 2011*. https://www.statistik-nord.de/fileadmin/Dokumente/Sonderver%C3%B6ffentlichungen/Zensus/Zensus_2011_Metropolregion_Hamburg_endErgebnisse.pdf

Statistisches Amt für Hamburg und Schleswig-Holstein. (2018). *Sozialversicherungspflichtig Beschäftigte in Hamburg am 30. Juni 2017*. www.statistik-nord.de/fileadmin/Dokumente/Statistische_Berichte/arbeit_und_soziales/A_VI_5_vj_HuS/A_VI_5_vj172_HH.pdf

Statistisches Amt für Hamburg und Schleswig-Holstein. (2020). *Statistisches Jahrbuch Hamburg 2019/2020*. www.hamburg.de/contentblob/1005676/e93bee7f01624bcadfd70efe661d6e28/data/statistisches-jahrbuch-hamburg.pdf

Statistisches Amt für Hamburg und Schleswig-Holstein. (2023). *Bevölkerungsentwicklung in Hamburg 2022*. Report No. AI1-j22HH. https://www.statistik-nord.de/fileadmin/Dokumente/Statistische_Berichte/bevoelkerung/A_I_1_j_H/A_I_1_j22_HH_Korrektur.pdf

Tinsley, H. E., Tinsley, D. J., & Croskeys, C. E. (2002). Park usage, social milieu, and psychosocial benefits of park use reported by older urban park users from four ethnic groups. *Leisure Sciences*, *24*(2), 199–218. https://doi.org/10.1080/01490400252900158

Tröger, J., Klack, M., Pätzold, A., Wendler, D., & Möller, C. (2016). *Das sind Deutschlands grünste Städte*. https://interaktiv.morgenpost.de/gruenste-staedte-deutschlands

White, M., Smith, A., Humphryes, K., Pahl, S., Snelling, D., & Depledge, M. (2010). Blue space: The importance of water for preference, affect, and restorativeness ratings of natural and built scenes. *Journal of Environmental Psychology*, *30*(4), 482–493. https://doi.org/10.1016/j.jenvp.2010.04.004

Yeager, D. S., Krosnick, J. A., Chang, L., Javitz, H. S., Levendusky, M. S., Simpser, A., & Wang, R. (2011). Comparing the accuracy of RDD telephone surveys and internet surveys conducted with probability and non-probability samples. *Public Opinion Quarterly*, *75*(4), 709–747. https://doi.org/10.1093/poq/nfr020

Zhao, Y., van den Berg, P. E. W., Ossokina, I. V., & Arentze, T. A. (2024). How do urban parks, neighborhood open spaces, and private gardens relate to individuals' subjective well-being: Results of a structural equation model. *Sustainable Cities and Society*, *101*, 105094. https://doi.org/10.1016/j.scs.2023.105094

3 Use of neighbourhood green spaces

Both the availability and use of green spaces in urban neighbourhoods can vary depending on the type of space. This study provides insights into four natural areas typically found in urban neighbourhoods: parks, waterfronts, fields and meadows, and woodlands, which are common in urban landscapes, at least in temperate regions such as central Europe.

The accessibility of green spaces in the neighbourhood is defined by the time it takes to walk to them. Respondents were asked whether they had access to any of the four types of green spaces within a 15-minute walk of their home. It was preferred to ask about accessibility in terms of time rather than distance (e.g. within 500 metres or 1 kilometres of home). This approach aims to minimise bias related to the health status and therefore walking speed of urban dwellers, so that accessibility within a 15-minute walk is more comparable across respondents. Using the 15-minute walk from home as a measure of accessibility attempts to capture the concept of the '15-minute city', as known in countries such as China (Weng et al., 2019) or France (Willsher, 2020). This concept of urban living emphasises the ability of city dwellers to reach essential facilities, including green spaces, within a short 15-minute walk.

Urban *parks* are often the focus of analyses of urban green spaces (Chiesura, 2004; Irvine et al., 2013; Kaspar, 2012; Mak & Jim, 2019; Pinto et al., 2021; Tinsley et al., 2002). With their variety of naturalness, biodiversity, and size, urban parks serve as multifunctional places to experience nature in the urban environment, bridging the gap between everyday life and moments of relaxation (Kaspar, 2012). Most respondents in the current study indicated that they can reach a park within a 15-minute walk, and only 11% do not live in such close proximity to parks.

There is a substantial body of literature on the positive effects of urban blue spaces on general well-being and health (see e.g. Gascon et al., 2017, for an overview), similar to those described for green spaces in Chapter 1. Indeed, it appears that blue spaces, which are fully integrated into the built environment and occur predominantly in urban contexts, receive roughly the same response from respondents in terms of attractiveness as purely green

DOI: 10.4324/9781003546146-4

environments (White et al., 2010). In this study, *waterfront areas* such as lake and river banks are considered green spaces because in cities in temperate regions such as central Europe, these areas are often accompanied by vegetation, including bushes, shrubs, trees, and lawns. According to the data, 29% of respondents say that there are no water areas within a 15-minute walk of their home, with this proportion being significantly higher in Cologne (33%) than in Hamburg (24%).

While *fields, meadows, and woods* are typically associated with rural landscapes, they are not uncommon in urban areas, especially on the outskirts of large cities. This is supported by statistical data, showing that 8% of the area of Hamburg and 18% of the area of Cologne consists of woodland, while agricultural land, comprising mainly fields and meadows, accounts for 16% in Cologne and 23% in Hamburg, all within the city boundaries and excluding the outskirts (Kölner Statistische Nachrichten, 2023; Statistisches Amt für Hamburg und Schleswig-Holstein, 2021). The respondents' data also support the availability of fields, meadows, and woods in urban areas, as only 35% of respondents said that they have no access to fields or meadows, and 42% have no access to woods within a 15-minute walk of their home. These natural areas tend to be more biodiverse and may even contribute more to overall well-being than less biodiverse urban green elements (see, e.g. Carrus et al., 2015; Schebella et al., 2019).

The reasons for visiting green spaces, which will be discussed in more detail later, were asked only if respondents reported using the green space at least several times a month. The reasons for use recorded in the survey are the same for all four green spaces in the neighbourhood (see Figure 3.1)

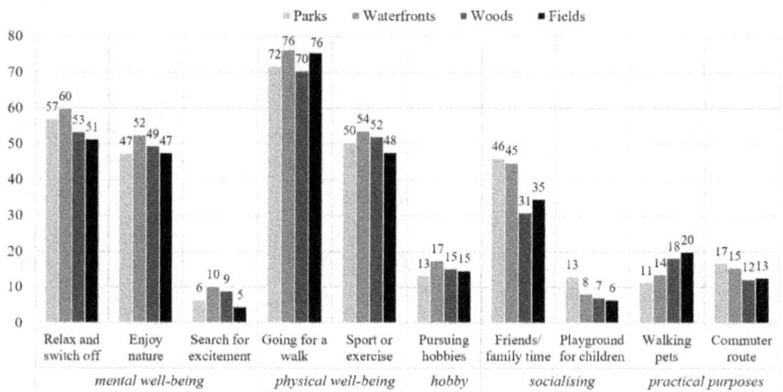

Figure 3.1 Reasons for using parks, waterfront areas, woods, and fields or meadows

Notes: Estimates design weighted; survey data from Hamburg and Cologne, collected in 2020/2021. Based on respondents who visit green spaces monthly or more often: parks ($N = 1092$), waterfronts ($N = 774$), woods ($N = 562$), and fields or meadows ($N = 528$).

and include motives that can be broadly grouped into five main categories, although the boundaries among these categories are not always clear, and some motives could be assigned to more than one category.[1]

The first category of use motives relates to the intentional promotion of mental well-being, such as using green spaces to relax, to experience something exciting, or to consciously enjoy nature. Motives for using green spaces to intentionally improve physical well-being include going for a walk or taking part in sporting activities. Research suggests that motives that consciously focus on the restorative qualities of the environment, such as those in the first two categories in Figure 3.1, are likely to be more relevant to the well-being of city dwellers than motives that are not directly related to restoration (Carrus et al., 2015).

The category of using green spaces for hobbies stands alone, as it can vary greatly depending on the specific interests of the respondents. The reasons for using green spaces for social purposes include spending time with family and friends or doing activities with children. The final category includes two more pragmatic reasons for using green spaces, namely as an exercise area for pets, such as walking dogs, or as a commuting route to reach other destinations. For each green space, respondents were given the opportunity to add other reasons for use. However, these rather sporadic mentions did not show any substantial prevalence and are not reported in this study.

Figure 3.1 illustrates the motives for using four types of green spaces in urban residential areas. Common motives for all green spaces, such as walking, relaxing, engaging in sports or exercise, and simply enjoying nature, appear to be the main drivers for using urban nature. In contrast, activities such as seeking exciting experiences, using children's playgrounds, or using green spaces as transport routes are less valued overall.

Walking is the most popular reason for using natural amenities in the neighbourhood, regardless of whether they are parks, waterfronts, woods, or fields. This tendency to walk is closely followed by a related motive: using nearby nature for relaxation. This is in line with existing research showing that walking (Irvine et al., 2013; Pinto et al., 2021), relaxing (Chiesura, 2004), and enjoying fresh air (Breuste & Artmann, 2020, p. 422) are among the most common motivations for visiting urban green spaces, especially parks. Sporting activities and enjoying nature are slightly less common motivations for all outdoor activities. Spending time with family or friends is another common reason for visiting neighbourhood nature, although it is much less common for woods.

The order of the other reasons varies considerably across the four types of nature offerings. In the case of urban parks and fields or meadows, the least frequently cited reason for using them is the search for exciting experiences. For waterfront areas and woods, the least frequent reason is to play with children. This could be due to the fact that there are usually only limited play areas available on riverbanks or in wooded areas, or that families prefer alternative recreational areas because it is difficult to supervise children in waterfront or wooded areas.

When comparing the use patterns of different types of green spaces, waterfront areas are the most popular for activities that should directly promote mental well-being,[2] as well as for sports and hobbies. Parks, on the other hand, are used more for social activities, such as meeting family or friends, and for children to play. In particular, parks and waterfronts are important places for socialising with friends and family, while woods or fields seem to play a subordinate role in such gatherings. A contrasting pattern is observed for walking animals: larger green spaces such as woods and fields are used more often for this purpose than parks and waterfront areas. This could be due to the stricter regulations in parks and waterfront areas, which restrict the free running of dogs. In contrast, parks and waterfront areas are used more often as commuting routes, which is in line with previous research (Breuste & Artmann, 2020, p. 409), probably due to their better developed infrastructure compared to woods or fields, making them convenient shortcuts for navigating within the city.

Use of green residential areas by life course phase and social class

As shown in Chapter 1, there are differences in the beneficial effects and use of green spaces across the life course and across social classes. In the following, patterns of use of neighbourhood green spaces are analysed from these two perspectives.

Table 3.1 illustrates how the life course phases are defined in this study. The *young adult phase* includes people aged 18–34 without children. At this stage in their lives, 38% of respondents are still living with their parents, suggesting that individuals are unlikely to be as centrally located as the 62% who have already moved out of their parents' home. This may also mean that

Table 3.1 Definition of life course phases

	Young adult phase	*Family phase*	*Midlife phase*	*Senior phase*
Age of respondents	18–34 years	> 18 years	35–65 years	> 65 years
Age of children in the household	No children	Under 10 years or expecting childbirth within 6 months	No children or with child(ren) 10 years + without younger siblings	
No. of persons	169	240	994	437

the availability of green spaces varies at this stage. Distinct patterns of green space use are expected in this life course phase, possibly with a focus on socialising with peers or sporting activities.

The *family phase* includes respondents living with children under ten or expecting a child. The age limit of ten years was chosen because children up to this age are less independent, and their parents' lives are often very child-centred. Due to the dependency of children on their parents, the age of the respondents themselves is less relevant, so that the age of the respondents, with an average age of 42, does not play a major role in the definition of this life course phase.

The *midlife phase* comprises all adults who either are childless and over 34 years of age or live with children aged 10 or over in the same household without younger siblings. The average age at this stage of life is 53. At this point in life, parents are more independent once again, although those with children may still consider their children's needs in relation to green spaces, such as safety when letting their children play alone.

The *senior phase* includes all respondents over the age of 65 without children or with children over the age of ten without younger siblings. In this life course phase, different patterns of green space usage may emerge, as needs may change compared to the previous phases of the life course. Both health-promoting and socialising components could play a greater role.

Table 3.2 shows the classification of social classes used in this study. Although it could be argued that the division of society into classes seems somewhat outdated in contemporary times, it is important to highlight that there are considerable disparities across social classes, as demonstrated by the research findings in Chapter 1. Neglecting these differences in the current study would contradict the existing scientific evidence. Thus, despite the prevalent belief that we live in a highly individualised society without class distinctions, empirical evidence from the research literature suggests the opposite.

To determine social classes, respondents were asked about their occupation, employment status, professional position, self-employment, and number of employees, both for themselves and for their partners in the same household. If information on occupation was available for both partners, the higher of the two social classes was defined as the social class of the household. In cases of unemployment or retirement, information on previous employment was used, as in such cases people may not necessarily lose status or change their lifestyle substantially, especially in the case of short-term unemployment. Occupations were coded according to the International Standard Classification of Occupations 2008 (ISCO08). Social classes were then defined using the Erikson–Goldthorpe–Portocarero (EGP) scheme (Erikson & Goldthorpe, 1992, 2002; Ganzeboom & Treiman, 1996). The categories 'farmers' and 'agricultural workers' were completely excluded from the analysis, as these

Table 3.2 Definition of social classes

	Higher-grade professionals	*Lower-grade professionals*	*Routine sales and service workers*	*Blue-collar workers*
Detailed coding according to the EGP-scheme (Erikson & Goldthorpe, 1992, 2002)	Professionals, administrators, and managers, higher grade (I)	Professionals, administrators, and managers, lower grade; technicians, higher grade (II) + Small employers (IVa)	Routine nonmanual employees, higher grade (IIIa) + Routine nonmanual employees, lower grade (IIIb)	Self-employed workers (IVb) + Skilled manual workers (VI) + Nonskilled manual workers (VIIa)
Occupational specification (Ganzeboom & Treiman, 1996)	Example: employers in large companies; upper level managers with more than ten subordinates	Example: associate professionals; lower level managers or small business owners with one to ten subordinates; higher-level sales functions	Example: regular office staff and sales staff	Example: self-employed without employees; craft workers; machine operators; elementary labourers; basic sales and service staff
No. of persons	296	618	600	326

Notes: The roman numerals refer to Erikson and Goldthorpe (2002).

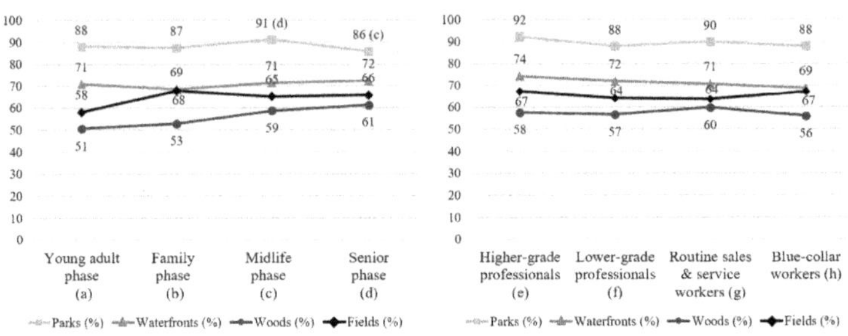

Figure 3.2 Availability of neighbourhood green spaces by life course phase (left) and social class (right)

Notes: Estimates design weighted; survey data from Hamburg and Cologne, collected in 2020/2021. Young adult phase ($N = 169$), family phase ($N = 240$), midlife phase ($N = 994$), and senior phase ($N = 437$). Higher-grade professionals ($N = 296$), lower-grade professionals ($N = 618$), routine sales and service workers ($N = 600$), and blue-collar workers ($N = 326$).

(a/b/c/d) significant difference ($p < 0.05$) between life course phases.

(e/f/g/h) significant difference ($p < 0.05$) between social classes.

groups are likely to have different patterns of availability and use of green spaces compared to other urban dwellers.[3]

Figure 3.2 shows the availability of four different types of green spaces in the neighbourhood by life course phase (left) and social class (right). Across all life course phases, parks are most likely to be available (86% to 91%), followed by waterfronts (69% to 72%) and fields (58% to 68%). In contrast, the likelihood of having woodland in the neighbourhood is the lowest across all life course phases, ranging from 51% to 61%. The only significant difference in the availability of green spaces is between the midlife and senior phases in relation to parks. A similar pattern can be observed in the availability of green spaces across social classes, with no significant differences among them. It therefore seems important to compare the patterns of green space use in the different life course phases and social classes in more detail.

Figure 3.3 zooms in on the variation in the frequency of use of neighbourhood green spaces, showing daily and weekly use together. In terms of park use, respondents in the family phase are significantly more likely to visit parks on a weekly or daily basis than all other life course phases. The use of fields is also significantly higher in the family phase than in the young adult and midlife phases. Although this difference is less pronounced and not statistically significant compared to the senior phase, the pattern indicates a more frequent weekly use of all green spaces in the family phase, with the exception of waterfront areas. This supports previous research (Łaszkiewicz et al., 2023) showing that respondents with children tend to use urban green spaces more frequently than those without children. In general, all types of green spaces

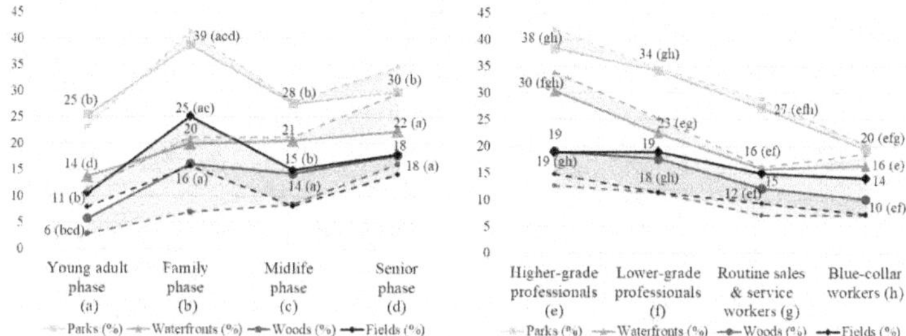

Figure 3.3 Combined daily and weekly usage of neighbourhood green spaces by life course phase (left) and social class (right). Dashed lines: exclusively those without private gardens or terraces

Notes: Estimates design weighted; survey data from Hamburg and Cologne, collected in 2020/2021. Young adult phase (N = 169), family phase (N = 240), midlife phase (N = 994), and senior phase (N = 437). Higher-grade professionals (N = 296), lower-grade professionals (N = 618), routine sales and service workers (N = 600), and blue-collar workers (N = 326).

(a/b/c/d) significant difference ($p < 0.05$) between life course phases.

(e/f/g/h) significant difference ($p < 0.05$) between social classes.

are used least in the young adult phase compared to other life course phases, with woods showing the clearest difference. Overall, there are no significant differences in the combined daily and weekly usage of neighbourhood green spaces between the midlife and senior phases.

Looking at the patterns of use in the different social classes (see Figure 3.3, right), there are significant differences, especially between the two upper and the two lower social classes. This is in line with previous findings (Pinto et al., 2021), suggesting that more affluent urban residents are more likely to use urban green spaces, particularly urban parks. Higher- and lower-grade professionals are significantly more likely to use parks and woods at least weekly than routine sales and service workers or blue-collar workers. There is also a significant difference between the two lower social classes when it comes to parks, with blue-collar workers the least likely to use parks weekly or daily. Waterfront areas are used at least weekly significantly more often by higher-grade professionals than by all other social classes. However, there are no significant differences in the frequency of use across social classes for fields.

In addition to evaluating the accessibility of neighbourhood green spaces, as shown earlier, it is important to look more closely at the availability of private green spaces in different life course phases and social classes. For example, individuals who do not have access to a private garden may be more dependent on neighbourhood green spaces to enjoy nature. In Figure 3.3, the dashed lines represent combined daily and weekly frequency of use for individuals without access to a private garden or terrace. Park use intensifies in

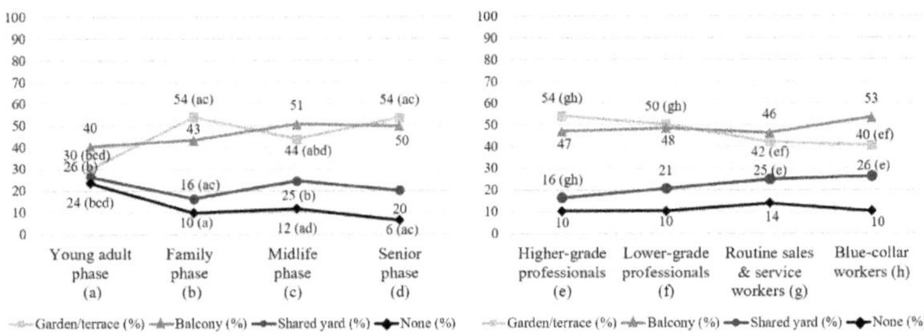

Figure 3.4 Availability of private and shared green spaces by life course phase (left) and social class (right)

Notes: Estimates design weighted; survey data from Hamburg and Cologne, collected in 2020/2021. Young adult phase ($N = 169$), family phase ($N = 240$), midlife phase ($N = 994$), and senior phase ($N = 437$). Higher-grade professionals ($N = 296$), lower-grade professionals ($N = 618$), routine sales and service workers ($N = 600$), and blue-collar workers ($N = 326$).

(a/b/c/d) significant difference ($p < 0.05$) between life course phases.

(e/f/g/h) significant difference ($p < 0.05$) between social classes.

the family and senior phases for those without access to a garden or terrace. Additionally, those in the senior phase without a garden or terrace tend to visit the waterfront areas more frequently. Across all social classes, the frequency of visits to both parks and waterfront areas is higher for those who lack private gardens and terraces.

Figure 3.4 also shows the availability of private and shared green spaces, including gardens and terraces, balconies, shared yards, or lack thereof, by life course phase (left) and social class (right).

Compared with the young adult and midlife phases, individuals in the family and senior phases are significantly more likely to have their own garden or terrace. Conversely, shared yards are more common in the young adult and midlife phases, with a statistically significant difference observed only in contrast to the family phase, but not to the senior phase. Balconies, on the other hand, are more common in the later phases of the life course (i.e. in the midlife and in senior phases), although no significant differences can be observed here. Compared to all other life course phases, the lack of shared and private green spaces is significantly higher in the young adult phase.

The availability of private or shared green spaces in the four social classes (see Figure 3.4, right) shows a distinct contrast between the upper and lower socio-economic groups. Members of both the higher- and lower-grade professionals are significantly more likely to have their own garden or terrace. Conversely, routine sales and service workers and blue-collar workers are more likely to have a shared yard, although the difference is statistically significant compared to the higher- but not to the lower-grade professionals. Balconies are slightly more common among blue-collar workers, but no statistically

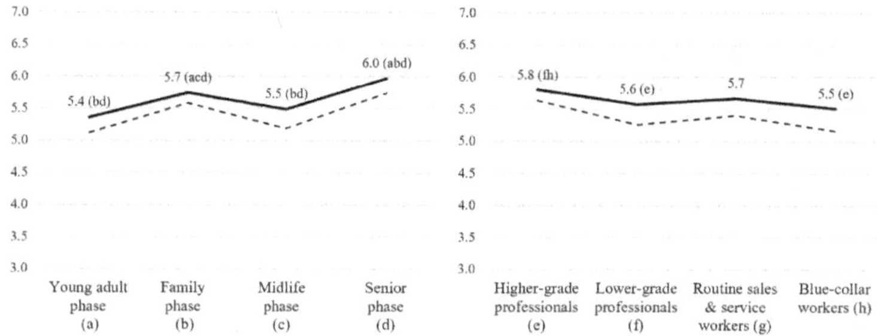

Figure 3.5 Satisfaction with green spaces in the neighbourhood by life course phase (left) and social class (right). Dashed lines: exclusively those without private gardens or terraces

Notes: Estimates design weighted; survey data from Hamburg and Cologne, collected in 2020/2021. Young adult phase ($N = 169$), family phase ($N = 240$), midlife phase ($N = 994$), and senior phase ($N = 437$). Higher-grade professionals ($N = 296$), lower-grade professionals ($N = 618$), routine sales and service workers ($N = 600$), and blue-collar workers ($N = 326$).

(a/b/c/d) significant difference ($p < 0.05$) between life course phases.

(e/f/g/h) significant difference ($p < 0.05$) between social classes.

significant differences were found across social classes in terms of balcony ownership.

Given that there are differences in the availability and use of accessible green spaces, it is not surprising that there are also differences in satisfaction with neighbourhood green spaces across life course phases and social classes, as shown in Figure 3.5. In this study, satisfaction with green spaces was measured by asking respondents: 'How satisfied are you with the availability of nature in your neighbourhood?'. Participants rated their satisfaction with nature on a seven-point Likert scale, ranging from *completely dissatisfied* to *completely satisfied.* The first thing that stands out is that satisfaction with nature is lower across all life course phases and social classes if people do not have their own garden or terrace (dashed lines in Figure 3.5).

Satisfaction with neighbourhood green spaces is highest in the senior phase and significantly exceeds all other life course phases. This is closely followed by the family phase, which, in line with previous research (Kearney, 2006), shows significantly higher levels of satisfaction than the young adult and midlife phases. These discrepancies across life course phases could be another indicator of differences in the availability and use of green spaces. Additionally, it might be important to capture the specific purposes for which different green spaces are used in each life course phase – an issue that will be discussed in more detail in the following sections.

Compared to the life course differences, the variations in satisfaction across social classes (see Figure 3.5, right) are less pronounced but still show some significant differences. As might be expected, higher-grade professionals are the most satisfied with the green spaces in their neighbourhood. However, this discrepancy is not significant when compared to routine sales and service workers. This raises the question of why the latter have such a high level of satisfaction with green spaces. In order to better understand this aspect and the overall sources of satisfaction with neighbourhood nature in the different social classes, the following analysis examines the activities that take place in the different types of green spaces in the different social classes.

Parks

Figure 3.6 illustrates the predominant motives for using parks in the four life course phases. Regardless of the life course phase, parks are essential for motives that aim to enhance mental and physical well-being. Activities such as walking, enjoying nature, or relaxing are very popular in all phases. Although parks serve practical functions, such as walking dogs or commuting, these motives are less common compared to activities intended to consciously increase well-being.

In the family phase, parks are visited more frequently for social activities, such as meeting family or friends, compared to all other life course phases. This difference is particularly significant compared to respondents in the

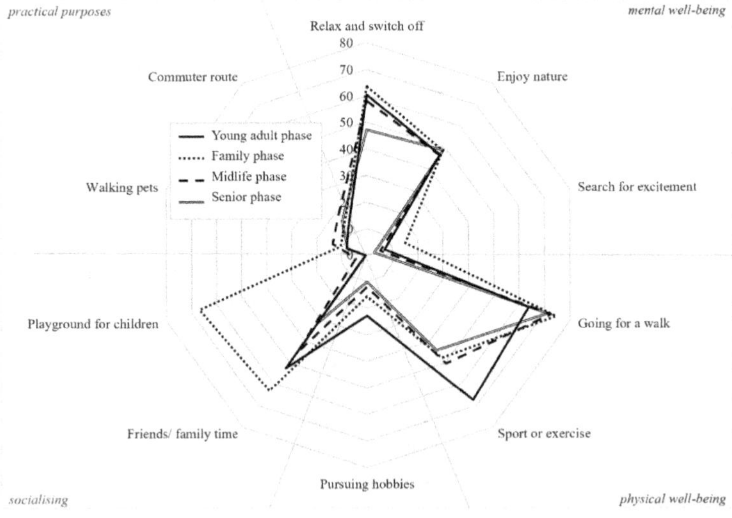

Figure 3.6 Reasons for using *parks* by life course phase

Notes: Estimates design weighted; survey data from Hamburg and Cologne, collected in 2020/2021. Based on respondents who visit parks monthly or more often: Young adult phase ($N = 94$), family phase ($N = 167$), midlife phase ($N = 595$), and senior phase ($N = 236$).

midlife ($p = 0.001$) and senior phases ($p = 0.000$). Additionally, parks in the family phase are significantly more likely to be seen as a place to experience exciting activities compared to all other groups ($p < 0.1$). As expected, parks in the family phase serve as playgrounds for children, which is not observed in the other life course phases due to the absence of younger children. In the young adult phase, parks are used significantly more often for sport or exercise than in any other life course phase ($p < 0.05$), and for hobbies than in the midlife ($p = 0.015$) and senior phases ($p = 0.009$). Older adults in the senior phase tend to use parks significantly less for relaxation ($p < 0.1$) and for social activities such as meeting family or friends ($p < 0.01$) than other life course phases.

Figure 3.7 also shows a ranking of the reasons for using parks in the four life course phases. This makes it easier to identify differences in the importance of the reasons for using parks in the different life course phases and goes beyond a simple comparison of the actual frequency of park visits attributed to these reasons.

Walking and relaxing are consistently in the top three reasons for using parks across all life course phases, as in previous studies (Breuste & Artmann, 2020, p. 434; Chiesura, 2004; Irvine et al., 2013; Pinto et al., 2021). With the exception of the young adult phase, walking is the main reason for visiting urban parks. For younger adults, on the other hand, sport and exercise are the

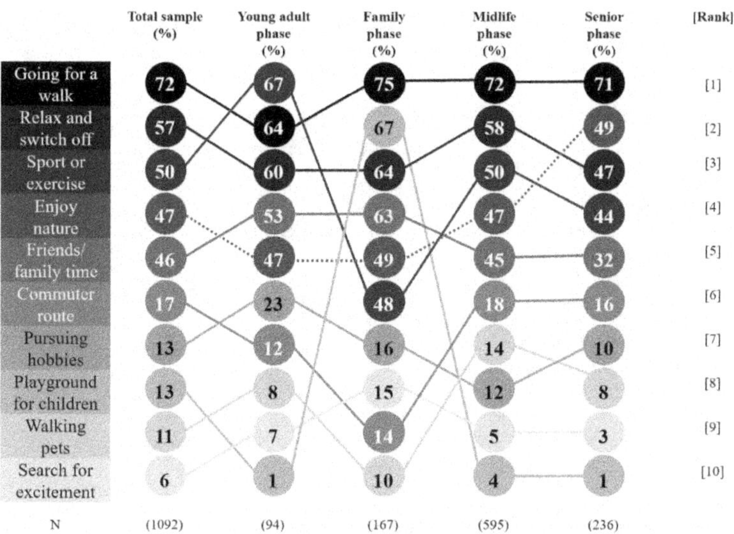

Figure 3.7 Ranking of reasons for using *parks* at different life course phases

Notes: Estimates design weighted; survey data from Hamburg and Cologne, collected in 2020/2021.

most common activities. A notable observation is the comparatively lower importance of sport and exercise in the family phase, which ranks much lower than in the other life course phases. The importance of enjoying nature as a motive for using parks increases over the life course and peaks in the senior phase. Meeting family or friends is more important in the young adult and family phases but gradually loses importance in the midlife and senior phases. Similarly, the importance of hobbies decreases over the life course, with a slight comeback in the senior phase.

Across all life course phases, exciting experiences and playgrounds for children (except in the family phase for the latter) are among the least prioritised reasons for using parks. Walking pets ranks third to last in the young adult and senior phases, with no distinction between these two phases in the overall bottom three. The use of parks for walking pets increases in the midlife phase and decreases again in the senior phase. In the family phase, experiencing something exciting has a relatively high value compared to the other life course phases; This may be due to the fact that people in the family phase, who typically spend most of their time with their children and engage less in their usual activities such as employment, visit parks to introduce variety to their predominantly routine-orientated lifestyles.

Figure 3.8 illustrates the reasons for using parks in different social classes. Similar to the life course phases, reasons related to mental and physical

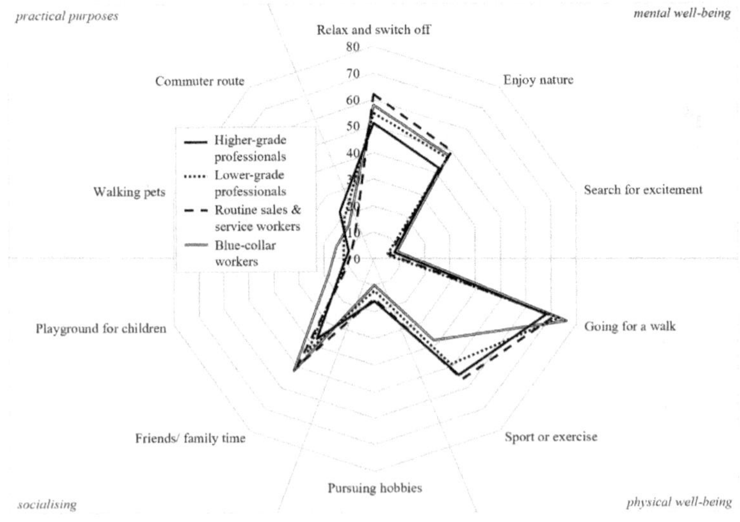

Figure 3.8 Reasons for using *parks* by social class

Notes: Estimates design weighted; survey data from Hamburg and Cologne, collected in 2020/2021. Based on respondents who visit parks monthly or more often: Higher-grade professionals ($N = 202$), lower-grade professionals ($N = 384$), routine sales and service workers ($N = 343$), and blue-collar workers ($N = 163$).

well-being, such as relaxing, enjoying nature, or going for a walk, are highly prioritised across all social classes, while practical purposes and hobbies are less common.

No significant differences were found across social classes for reasons such as enjoying nature, walking, practising hobbies, or playing with children. However, blue-collar workers are significantly less likely to use parks for sport and exercise compared to all better-off social classes ($p < 0.05$). Conversely, they are slightly more likely to use parks to seek out exciting experiences, although this difference is significant only when compared to lower-grade professionals ($p = 0.057$). Parks are also used more frequently for relaxation by the two lower social classes, although a significant difference can only be observed among the higher-grade professionals and the routine sales and service workers ($p = 0.036$). For meeting family and friends, blue-collar workers use parks more often than both higher- ($p = 0.014$) and lower-grade professionals ($p = 0.086$).

Looking at the ranking of park use purposes (which are not shown in an additional figure due to minor differences), walking, relaxing, and practising sport or exercise are consistently in the top three priorities across all social classes. However, there is one exception: among blue-collar workers, meeting family and friends is prioritised over sport or exercise.

Waterfront areas

Figure 3.9 illustrates the reasons for using waterfront areas in the different life course phases. In terms of enhancing mental well-being, there are no significant differences across the life course phases in terms of enjoying nature. However, waterfront areas are used significantly less for relaxation in the senior phase than in the young adult ($p = 0.017$) and midlife phases ($p = 0.009$). Additionally, water areas are used significantly more often to experience excitement in the family phase than in the midlife ($p = 0.015$) and senior phases ($p = 0.008$). In terms of physical well-being, the young adult phase shows a significantly lower use of waterfront areas for walking ($p < 0.1$), and a significantly higher frequency of practising sport or exercise ($p < 0.1$) compared to all other life course phases.

Compared to all other groups, the senior phase uses waterfront areas significantly less for hobbies ($p < 0.01$) and as travel routes ($p < 0.1$). They are also used less frequently for meeting family or friends in both the midlife and senior phases compared to the young adult ($p < 0.05$) and family phases ($p < 0.001$). As might be expected, the use of waterfronts as playgrounds for children is most pronounced in the family phase. In addition, the use of waterfronts for walking animals is significantly higher in the family phase than in the young adult ($p = 0.051$) and senior phases ($p = 0.043$).

Figure 3.10 shows the ranking of reasons for using waterfront areas in different life course phases. In both the young adult and midlife phases, activities

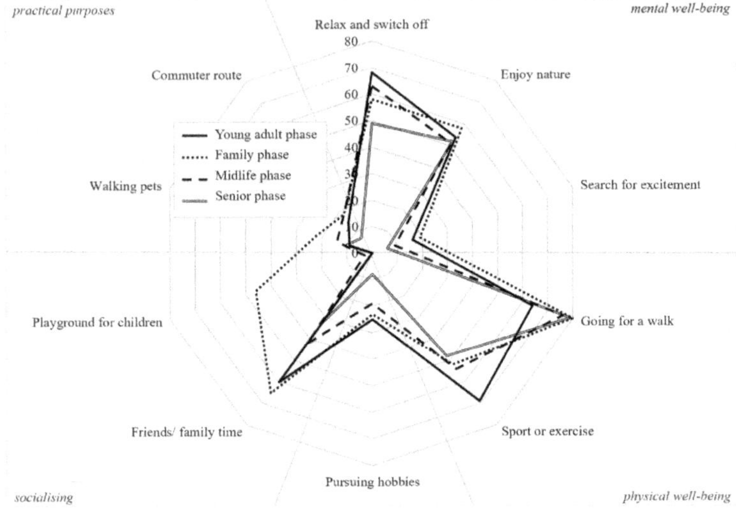

Figure 3.9 Reasons for using *waterfront areas* by life course phase

Notes: Estimates design weighted; survey data from Hamburg and Cologne, collected in 2020/2021. Based on respondents who visit waterfront areas monthly or more often: Young adult phase ($N = 74$), family phase ($N = 106$), midlife phase ($N = 432$), and senior phase ($N = 162$).

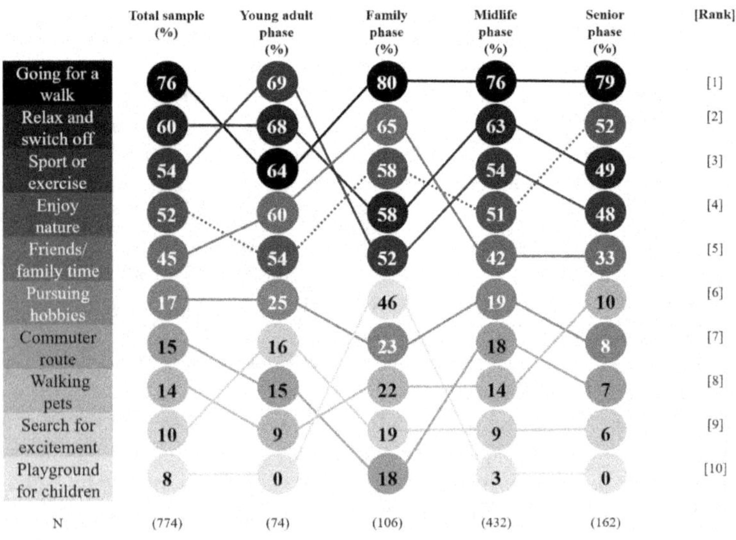

Figure 3.10 Ranking of reasons for using *waterfront areas* at different life course phases

Notes: Estimates design weighted; survey data from Hamburg and Cologne, collected in 2020/2021.

such as walking, relaxing, and engaging in sport or exercise are among the top three reasons for using waterfront areas. Conversely, in the family phase, meeting family or friends and enjoying nature, in addition to walking, are the most common reasons. According to prior research (Breuste & Artmann, 2020, p. 434), walking and meeting other people were the most common reasons for visiting urban waterfronts. Notably, the importance of enjoying nature increases steadily over the life course, and is one of the top two reasons for using waterfront areas in the senior phase. Prior research has also demonstrated that experiencing the beauty of nature is one of the main motivations for using urban waterfronts (Breuste & Artmann, 2020, p. 434). The importance of sport or exercise is highest in the young adult phase and decreases substantially in the family phase.

The reasons for using waterfront areas by social class are shown in Figure 3.11. In terms of mental well-being, blue-collar workers generally use waterfront areas more frequently than higher social classes. In particular, they use them significantly more often to enjoy nature than all other social classes ($p < 0.05$). They are also significantly more likely to use waterfronts for relaxation compared to higher- ($p = 0.011$) and lower-grade professionals ($p = 0.053$). Routine sales and service workers are also significantly more likely to use waterfronts for relaxation than higher-grade professionals

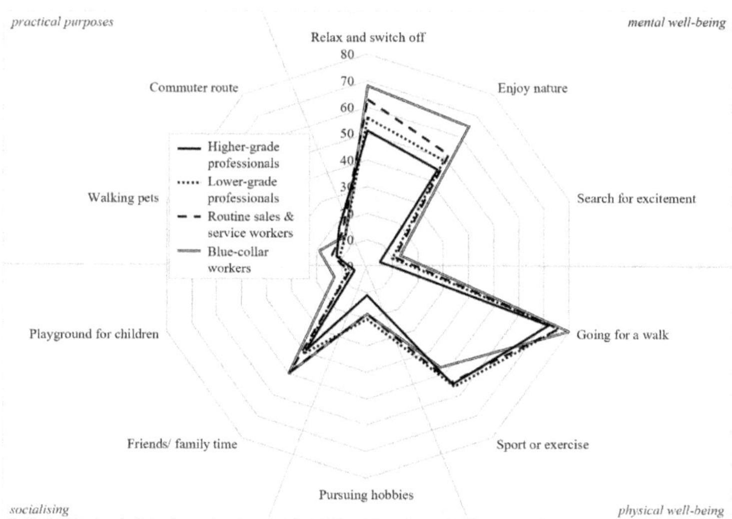

Figure 3.11 Reasons for using *waterfront areas* by social class

Notes: Estimates design weighted; survey data from Hamburg and Cologne, collected in 2020/2021. Based on respondents who visit waterfront areas monthly or more often: Higher-grade professionals ($N = 155$), lower-grade professionals ($N = 269$), routine sales and service workers ($N = 222$), and blue-collar workers ($N = 128$).

($p = 0.045$). The difference in use for excitement is significant only between blue-collar workers and higher-grade professionals ($p = 0.066$).

There are no significant differences in the use of waterfront areas across social classes in terms of physical well-being motives, such as walks, sport, or exercise. There are also no significant differences in terms of social and practical purposes, such as meeting family and friends or using waterfronts as travel routes. Blue-collar workers use waterfront areas significantly more frequently for playing with children compared to higher- ($p = 0.091$) and lower-grade professionals ($p = 0.06$), and they use these areas significantly more often for walking animals compared to lower-grade professionals ($p = 0.082$).

In the ranking of usage preferences (not shown in an additional figure due to minor differences), walking and relaxing are among the top three reasons across all social classes. Enjoying nature and meeting family or friends are prioritised higher by blue-collar workers compared to other social classes, while sport or exercise ranks lower. Exciting experiences and playgrounds for children are consistently ranked lowest across all social classes.

Woods

Preferences for using woods according to life course phase are shown in Figure 3.12. With regard to increasing mental well-being, woods are used

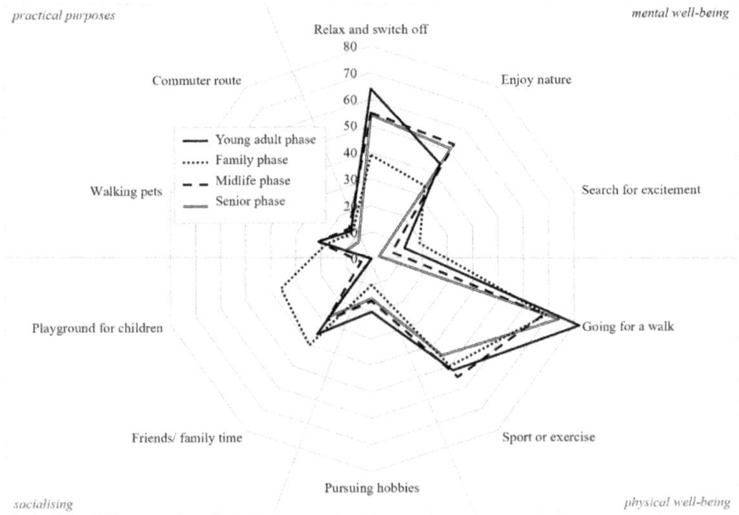

Figure 3.12 Reasons for using *woods* by life course phase

Notes: Estimates design weighted; survey data from Hamburg and Cologne, collected in 2020/2021. Based on respondents who visit woods monthly or more often: Young adult phase ($N = 45$), family phase ($N = 77$), midlife phase ($N = 317$), and senior phase ($N = 123$).

significantly less frequently for enjoying nature in the family phase than in the midlife ($p = 0.011$) and senior phases ($p = 0.041$), and also significantly less often for relaxation than in all other life course phases ($p < 0.1$). Adults in the senior phase are significantly less likely to use woods to seek exciting experiences compared to all other phases ($p < 0.1$).

There are no significant differences across the life course phases in the reasons for visiting woods for walking, doing sports or exercise, practising hobbies, meeting family or friends, and using woods as a travel route. However, the young adult and senior phases use woods slightly more frequently for walking than the other two phases, while meeting family or friends in the woods occurs more frequently in the young adult and family phases. Sport or exercise and hobbies are also slightly more common reasons for visiting woods in the midlife and young adult phases. Using woods as playgrounds for children, on the other hand, predominates in the family phase. Walking animals in the woods is about equally common in the three younger life course phases and less common in the senior phase, although the difference is significant only in comparison with the midlife phase ($p = 0.043$). Similarly, using woods for commuting is less common in the senior phase than in the other three life course phases, although the difference is not significant.

In the ranking of preferences for using woods (not shown in an additional figure due to minor differences), walking is the top reason across all phases, which is in line with existing studies (Breuste & Artmann, 2020, p. 434; Jensen & Koch, 2004). Relaxation is the second most important reason for all life course phases except the family phase. Sport or exercise also ranks among the top three reasons in the young adult, family, and midlife phases, while it is surpassed by enjoying nature in the senior phase. In the family phase, meeting family or friends in the woods is the third most important reason, higher than in any other phase. The bottom three reasons – commuting, looking for something exciting, and using woods as playgrounds for children – do not differ across the young adult, midlife, and senior phases. In the family phase, on the other hand, reasons such as walking animals, using woods for commuting, and practising hobbies, are rated as the least important.

Figure 3.13 shows the preferences for using woods in different social classes. There are no significant differences across the social classes in terms of motives for enhancing mental well-being reasons, such as relaxing, enjoying nature, and seeking exciting experiences. However, with regard to physical well-being, blue-collar workers tend to use woods less frequently for walking, with this difference being significant only when compared to routine sales and service workers ($p = 0.069$) and lower-grade professionals ($p = 0.009$). The latter use woods significantly more often for sport and exercise than all other classes ($p < 0.05$). Similarly, they show the highest engagement in hobbies in woods, but with a significant difference only compared to routine sales and service workers ($p = 0.051$). Higher-grade professionals are more likely to use wooded areas as playgrounds for children, especially compared to

Figure 3.13 Reasons for using *woods* by social class

Notes: Estimates design weighted; survey data from Hamburg and Cologne, collected in 2020/2021. Based on respondents who visit woods monthly or more often: Higher-grade professionals ($N = 109$), lower-grade professionals ($N = 204$), routine sales and service workers ($N = 174$), and blue-collar workers ($N = 75$).

lower-grade professionals ($p = 0.052$) and routine sales and service workers ($p = 0.022$). There are no significant differences across social classes in the use of woods as meeting places for family and friends or for walking animals.

The ranking of use preferences is not shown in an additional figure, as there is little difference in the ranking across social classes. The most common reasons for using woods for all social classes are walking, relaxing, doing sport or exercise, and enjoying nature. Conversely, the three reasons at the bottom of the ranking – commuting, looking for exciting experiences, and using woods as playgrounds for children – are the least common across all social classes.

Fields and meadows

When visiting fields or meadows (Figure 3.14), there are no significant differences across the life course phases in terms of mental and physical well-being when relaxing, enjoying nature, and walking. The young adult phase tends to use fields or meadows more frequently to look for exciting experiences, while the senior phase shows significantly less engagement in this respect compared to all other phases ($p < 0.05$). Additionally, the young adult phase demonstrates a higher frequency of using fields or meadows for hobbies,

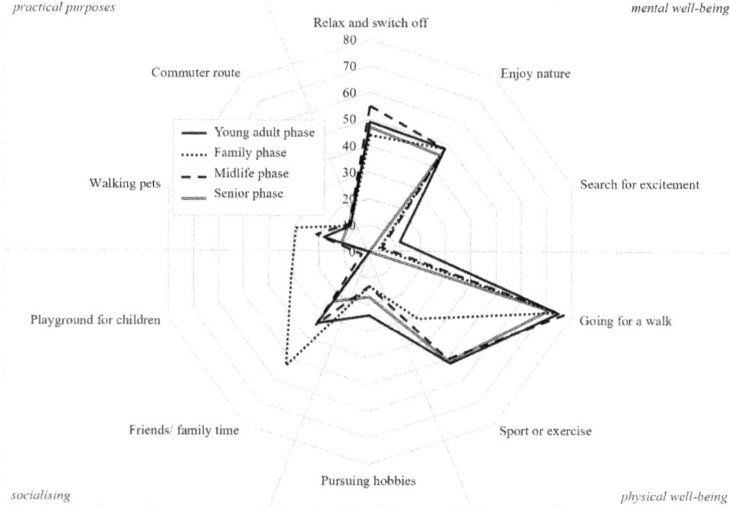

Figure 3.14 Reasons for using *fields or meadows* by life course phase

Notes: Estimates design weighted; survey data from Hamburg and Cologne, collected in 2020/2021. Based on respondents who visit fields or meadows monthly or more often: young adult phase ($N = 46$), family phase ($N = 78$), midlife phase ($N = 287$), and senior phase ($N = 117$).

although the difference is significant only when compared to the midlife phase ($p = 0.065$). In the family phase, fields and meadows are used significantly less often for sport or exercise than in the other phases ($p < 0.1$), while they are used significantly more often for meetings with family or friends than in all other phases ($p < 0.1$). Additionally, use for meeting family or friends is lowest in the senior phase, and also significantly less than in the midlife phase ($p = 0.055$). Furthermore, the senior phase uses fields and meadows for walking animals significantly less often than the family ($p = 0.018$) and midlife phases ($p = 0.082$). All life course phases use fields and meadows about equally often for commuting.

Looking at the top usage preferences (not shown in an additional figure due to minor differences), walking ranks highest across all life course phases. Compared to other neighbourhood green spaces, the ranking of use preferences for fields or meadows remains more stable across the life course phases, with the exception of the family phase.

Compared to other green spaces discussed in this analysis, there are fewer distinctions among social classes in the use of fields or meadows (Figure 3.15). The differences across social classes are minimal and not significant for almost all visit motives. The only significant difference is that routine sales and service workers are less likely to use fields and meadows for

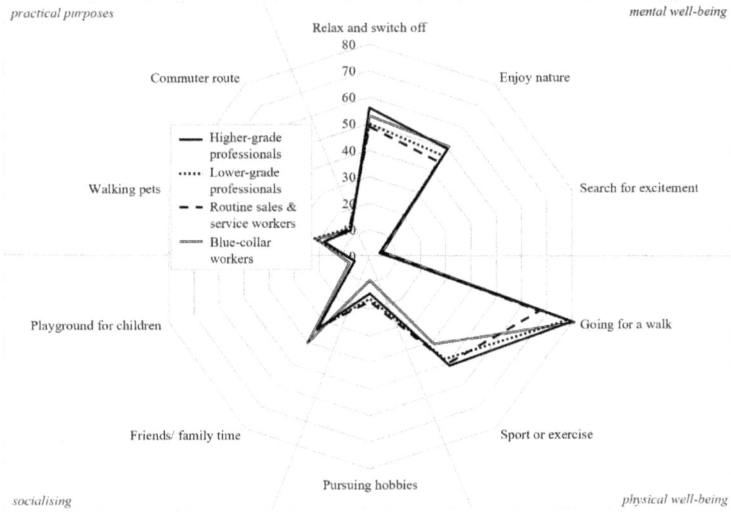

Figure 3.15 Reasons for using *fields or meadows* by social class

Notes: Estimates design weighted; survey data from Hamburg and Cologne, collected in 2020/2021. Based on respondents who visit fields or meadows monthly or more often: higher-grade professionals ($N = 90$), lower-grade professionals ($N = 187$), routine sales and service workers ($N = 160$), and blue-collar workers ($N = 91$).

walking than all other classes ($p < 0.1$). Additionally, blue-collar workers are on average slightly less likely to use fields and meadows for sport or exercise and hobbies, but more likely to use them for meeting family or friends.

The ranking of usage preferences (not shown in an additional figure due to minor differences) remains relatively stable compared to other neighbourhood green spaces. The three upper classes share a similar ranking: walks, relaxation, and sport or exercise are the top three preferences, while commuting, playgrounds for children, and looking for exciting experiences are at the bottom. There are also minimal differences among blue-collar workers, who prioritise, for example, enjoying nature over sport or exercise and hobbies.

Duration of stay in green spaces

Figure 3.16 shows the average duration in minutes for different types of green spaces during a typical visit in good weather, categorised by life course phase (left) and social class (right). The comparison of duration is based on median values, as these are less affected by outliers, especially in the case of time-based data. The average length of stay reported in previous studies on urban parks (Breuste & Artmann, 2020, p. 433 ff., 480) and woods (Jensen & Koch, 2004) roughly corresponds to the values observed in the current analysis.

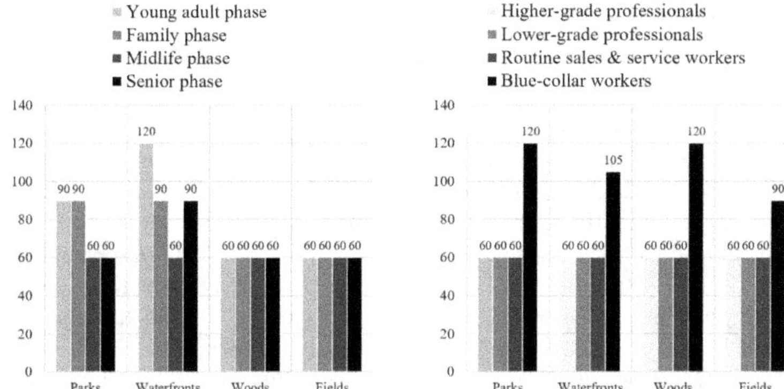

Figure 3.16 Median (in minutes) of the average time spent in green spaces during a typical visit in good weather, by life course phase (left) and social class (right)

Notes: Estimates design weighted; survey data from Hamburg and Cologne, collected in 2020/2021. Based on valid responses of respondents who visit the specific green spaces monthly or more often: young adult phase (N = 44–91), family phase (N = 75–165), midlife phase (N = 261–569), and senior phase (N = 107–223); Higher-grade professionals (N = 82–195), lower-grade professionals (N = 170–373), routine sales and service workers (N = 151–325), and blue-collar workers (N = 85–155).

The analysis of the life course phases shows that the time spent in woods and fields remains constant at one hour across all phases. However, there is a notable difference in parks, where respondents in the young adult and family phases spend an average of 90 minutes, half an hour longer than those in the midlife and senior phases. In addition, younger respondents tend to spend more time in waterfront areas (two hours on average), which may be due to the fact that they are less likely to have their own green space (see Figure 3.4). Additionally, activities such as sport and exercise as well as socialising with family or friends in parks and by the water are more common in the young adult and family phases (see Figures 3.7 and 3.10), which may contribute to longer stays.

Looking at the average time spent in green spaces by social class, there are minimal disparities between higher- and lower-grade professionals, and routine sales and service workers, who spend an average of one hour in the four green spaces. Conversely, blue-collar workers spend substantially more time, often twice as long, in public green spaces, suggesting a greater dependence on these areas. This pattern may be influenced by the lower likelihood of owning a garden (see Figure 3.4). Additionally, blue-collar workers are more likely to use public green spaces for social and recreational activities, such as meeting friends or family, and in particular to use parks and water areas for children or pets, which may contribute to longer durations.

Spatial distribution of green spaces on the basis of official statistics

As mentioned in Chapter 1, it is common to use objective measures of green space availability based on respondents' addresses to analyse various well-being benefits (Astell-Burt et al., 2014; Bertram & Rehdanz, 2015; Bijnens et al., 2020; Cervero & Duncan, 2003; Cohen-Cline et al., 2015; Coombes et al., 2010; Coppel & Wüstemann, 2017; Crouse et al., 2017; de Jong et al., 2012; De Vries et al., 2003; Demoury et al., 2017; Groenewegen et al., 2012; Hystad et al., 2014; James et al., 2016; Kearney, 2006; Kemperman & Timmermans, 2014; Krekel et al., 2016; Kweon et al., 2010; Lee et al., 2016; Lovasi et al., 2013; Maas et al., 2009; van den Berg et al., 2010; Wang et al., 2022; Wei et al., 2023; White et al., 2013; Wu et al., 2020; Zhang et al., 2017). Similarly, in the current study, respondents were asked to provide their addresses so that the spatial data on green space distribution could later be included in the analysis.

In order to analyse the spatial distribution of public green spaces, a multi-stage geocoding process was used for the respondents' addresses. Approximately 73% of respondents provided at least their street name, of which 40% also provided their house number. Where house numbers were missing, the geographical centre of the street was used as the reference point for geocoding. For streets with more than 300 house numbers ($N = 34$), the geocoding was refined using district information. The geocoding was carried out at the GESIS Leibniz Institute for the Social Sciences.

The resulting geocoordinates were linked to green space geodata for Cologne, Hamburg, and the surrounding federal states[4] using QGIS version 3.26.1. Buffer zones with a radius of 1,000 metres were then created around the geocoded addresses. This distance is roughly equivalent to a 15-minute walk at an average walking pace, and largely corresponds to the estimates of green space availability in the previous chapters. The percentage of green space within the 1,000 metre buffer around the respondents' addresses was then calculated.

Figure 3.17 illustrates the percentage of buffer zones within 1,000 metres of respondents' geocoded addresses that are covered by public green space, as determined using objective data based on official statistics. In terms of life course phases (left), the analysis shows that individuals in the young adult phase have significantly fewer green spaces within 1,000 metres of their home than the other life course phases, with only 16%. Conversely, people in the family phase have the highest proportion of green space at 22%. However, this difference is only statistically significant when compared with the young adult and midlife phases.

There are only minimal differences in the distribution of green spaces by social class (Figure 3.17, right), with the average availability across all classes remaining constant at between 19% and 20%. This corroborates the findings

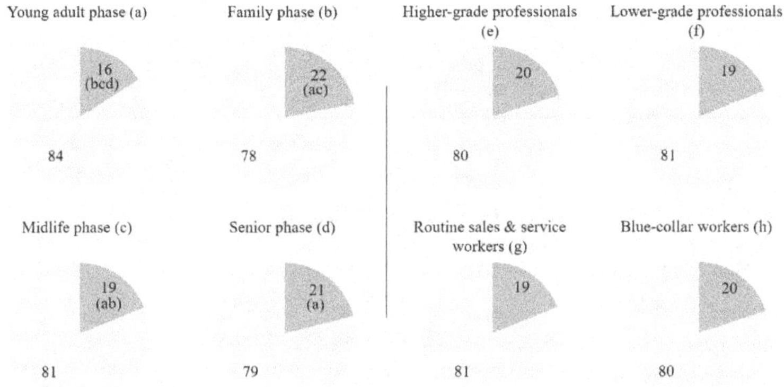

Figure 3.17 Extent (in %) of green spaces within the buffer zones of 1,000 metres around respondents' geocoded addresses, based on objective data

Notes: Estimates design weighted; survey data from Hamburg and Cologne, collected in 2020/2021. Young adult phase ($N = 169$), family phase ($N = 240$), midlife phase ($N = 994$), and senior phase ($N = 437$). Higher-grade professionals ($N = 296$), lower-grade professionals ($N = 618$), routine sales and service workers ($N = 600$), and blue-collar workers ($N = 326$).

(a/b/c/d) significant difference ($p < 0.05$) between life course phases.

(e/f/g/h) significant difference ($p < 0.05$) between social classes.

of Figure 3.2, which also shows no significant differences in the availability of public green spaces based on respondents' subjective assessments.

To assess the alignment between the subjective assessments and the objective data, Table 3.3 shows the pairwise Pearson's correlation coefficients. These coefficients show the relationships among the presence of green window views at home, the accessible green spaces within a 15-minute walk, and the objective data on green spaces within a 1,000-metre buffer zone around the respondent's geocoded address.

The presence of green window views at home is significantly positively correlated with the presence of public green spaces, whether subjectively or objectively assessed. However, parks are an exception, showing a weak negative correlation (–0.096, $p = 0.000$). This could be explained by the fact that parks are more likely to be found in central urban areas (Pearson's correlation of 0.199, $p = 0.000$, not shown in the table), which tend to be more densely developed, possibly leading to a negative correlation with the presence of green window views at home. There is also a significant positive correlation between the presence of parks and the availability of waterfronts, as they often coexist. However, there is a significant negative correlation between parks and the objectively measured amount of green space within the 1,000 metre buffer zone. The availability of waterfront areas, woods, and fields in the neighbourhood also shows positive and significant correlations with each

Table 3.3 Pairwise Pearson's correlation coefficients between the presence of green window views at home, accessible green spaces within a 15-minute walk, and objective data on green spaces within 1,000-metre buffer zones around respondents' geocoded addresses

	1	*2*	*3*	*4*	*5*
1. Green window view	1				
Availability of neighbourhood green spaces in 15-minute walking radius					
2. Parks	–0.096***	1			
3. Waterfront areas	0.083***	0.181***	1		
4. Woods	0.217***	0.015	0.273***	1	
5. Fields	0.128***	0.061**	0.116***	0.452***	1
Area within a 1,000-metre buffer zone around the respondent's geocoded address					
6. Green spaces	0.179***	–0.122***	0.006	0.214***	0.172***

Notes: Estimates design weighted; survey data from Hamburg and Cologne, collected in 2020/2021 ($N = 1840$).

*** $p < 0.001$, ** $p < 0.01$, * $p < 0.05$, + $p < 0.1$.

other. To summarise, subjective and objective measures of the availability of public green space do not differ substantially, and both measures could lead to similar results.[5]

Notes

1 Neither the factor analysis nor the cluster analysis was able to define clear motivation categories. The factor analysis carried out on all green spaces resulted in a single-factor solution with an eigenvalue of 2.9, while a two-factor solution would have resulted in an eigenvalue of less than 0.3. Various cluster analyses aimed at three-, four-, five-, and six-cluster solutions were inconclusive, as the reasons for use were mostly assigned to overlapping clusters. For this reason, the motives for use were categorised thematically to provide a better overview.

2 Here and in the rest of Chapter 3, the statements are based solely on the descriptive data provided by the respondents. The exact influence of each reason for use on the improvement of mental or physical well-being was not statistically tested.

3 As not all datasets allow such an analysis due to a lack of data to determine social class, the differences could also be analysed on the basis of respondents' education level (Pearson's correlation coefficient with socio-economic status 0.446, $p = 0.000$) or equivalised household income (Pearson's correlation coefficient with socio-economic status 0.289, $p = 0.000$). However, as the current study provides an accurate measurement of socio-economic status, and the differences are most pronounced here, this approach was chosen.

4 Data on public green spaces, community gardens, wooded and landscape conservation areas, cemeteries, nature reserves, grassland, moors, and heathlands:

https://geoportal-hamburg.de/geo-online, https://opendata.schleswig-holstein.de/dataset, www.geoportal.nrw/?activetab=map#/datasets/, www.umwelt.niedersachsen.de/startseite/service/umweltkarten/natur_amp_landschaft/besonders_geschutzte_teile_von_natur_und_landschaft, https://gdz.bkg.bund.de/index.php/default/open-data/corine-land-cover-5-ha-stand-2018-clc5–2018.html. Where data from different sources overlapped, areas were only included once in the analysis.

5 At city level, the correlation coefficients show only little variation.

References

Astell-Burt, T., Mitchell, R., & Hartig, T. (2014). The association between green space and mental health varies across the lifecourse. A longitudinal study. *Journal of Epidemiology and Community Health*, *68*(6), 578–583. https://doi.org/10.1136/jech-2013-203767

Bertram, C., & Rehdanz, K. (2015). The role of urban green space for human well-being. *Ecological Economics*, *120*, 139–152. https://doi.org/10.1016/j.ecolecon.2015.10.013

Bijnens, E. M., Derom, C., Thiery, E., Weyers, S., & Nawrot, T. S. (2020). Residential green space and child intelligence and behavior across urban, suburban, and rural areas in Belgium: A longitudinal birth cohort study of twins. *PLoS Medicine*, *17*(8), e1003213. https://doi.org/10.1371/journal.pmed.1003213

Breuste, J., & Artmann, M. (2020). Multi-functional urban green spaces. In J. Breuste, M. Artmann, C. Ioja, & S. Qureshi (Eds.), *Making green cities: Concepts, challenges and practice* (pp. 399–526). Springer.

Carrus, G., Scopelliti, M., Lafortezza, R., Colangelo, G., Ferrini, F., Salbitano, F., Agrimi, M., Portoghesi, L., Semenzato, P., & Sanesi, G. (2015). Go greener, feel better? The positive effects of biodiversity on the well-being of individuals visiting urban and peri-urban green areas. *Landscape and Urban Planning*, *134*, 221–228. https://doi.org/10.1016/j.landurbplan.2014.10.022

Cervero, R., & Duncan, M. (2003). Walking, bicycling, and urban landscapes: Evidence from the San Francisco Bay area. *American Journal of Public Health*, *93*(9), 1478–1483. https://doi.org/10.2105/ajph.93.9.1478

Chiesura, A. (2004). The role of urban parks for the sustainable city. *Landscape and Urban Planning*, *68*(1), 129–138. https://doi.org/10.1016/j.landurbplan.2003.08.003

Cohen-Cline, H., Turkheimer, E., & Duncan, G. E. (2015). Access to green space, physical activity and mental health: A twin study. *Journal of Epidemiology and Community Health*, *69*(6), 523–529. https://doi.org/10.1136/jech-2014-204667

Coombes, E., Jones, A. P., & Hillsdon, M. (2010). The relationship of physical activity and overweight to objectively measured green space accessibility and use. *Social Science & Medicine*, *70*(6), 816–822. https://doi.org/10.1016/j.socscimed.2009.11.020

Coppel, G., & Wüstemann, H. (2017). The impact of urban green space on health in Berlin, Germany: Empirical findings and implications for urban planning. *Landscape and Urban Planning*, *167*, 410–418. https://doi.org/10.1016/j.landurbplan.2017.06.015

Crouse, D. L., Pinault, L., Balram, A., Hystad, P., Peters, P. A., Chen, H., van Donkelaar, A., Martin, R. V., Ménard, R., Robichaud, A., & Villeneuve, P. J. (2017). Urban greenness and mortality in Canada's largest cities: A national cohort study. *The Lancet Planetary Health*, *1*(7), e289–e297. https://doi.org/10.1016/S2542-5196(17)30118-3

de Jong, K., Albin, M., Skärbäck, E., Grahn, P., & Björk, J. (2012). Perceived green qualities were associated with neighborhood satisfaction, physical activity, and general health: Results from a cross-sectional study in suburban and rural Scania, Southern Sweden. *Health & Place*, *18*(6), 1374–1380. https://doi.org/10.1016/j.healthplace.2012.07.001

Demoury, C., Thierry, B., Richard, H., Sigler, B., Kestens, Y., & Parent, M.-E. (2017). Residential greenness and risk of prostate cancer: A case-control study in Montreal, Canada. *Environment International*, *98*, 129–136. https://doi.org/10.1016/j.envint.2016.10.024

De Vries, S., Verheij, R. A., Groenewegen, P. P., & Spreeuwenberg, P. (2003). Natural environments – healthy environments? An exploratory analysis of the relationship between greenspace and health. *Environment and Planning A: Economy and Space*, *35*(10), 1717–1731. https://doi.org/10.1068/a35111

Erikson, R., & Goldthorpe, J. H. (1992). *The constant flux: A study of class mobility in industrial societies*. Clarendon Press.

Erikson, R., & Goldthorpe, J. H. (2002). Intergenerational inequality: A sociological perspective. *Journal of Economic Perspectives*, *16*(3), 31–44. https://doi.org/10.1257/089533002760278695

Ganzeboom, H. B. G., & Treiman, D. J. (1996). Internationally comparable measures of occupational status for the 1988 international standard classification of occupations. *Social Science Research*, *25*(3), 201–239. https://doi.org/10.1006/ssre.1996.0010

Gascon, M., Zijlema, W., Vert, C., White, M. P., & Nieuwenhuijsen, M. J. (2017). Outdoor blue spaces, human health and well-being: A systematic review of quantitative studies. *International Journal of Hygiene and Environmental Health*, *220*(8), 1207–1221. https://doi.org/10.1016/j.ijheh.2017.08.004

Groenewegen, P. P., van den Berg, A. E., Maas, J., Verheij, R. A., & de Vries, S. (2012). Is a green residential environment better for health? If so, why? *Annals of the Association of American Geographers*, *102*(5), 996–1003. https://doi.org/10.1080/00045608.2012.674899

Hystad, P., Davies, H. W., Frank, L., Van Loon, J., Gehring, U., Tamburic, L., & Brauer, M. (2014). Residential greenness and birth outcomes: Evaluating the influence of spatially correlated built-environment factors. *Environmental Health Perspectives*, *122*(10), 1095–1102. https://doi.org/10.1289/ehp.1308049

Irvine, K. N., Warber, S. L., Devine-Wright, P., & Gaston, K. J. (2013). Understanding urban green space as a health resource: A qualitative comparison of visit motivation and derived effects among park users in Sheffield, UK. *International Journal of Environmental Research and Public Health*, *10*(1), 417–442. https://doi.org/10.3390/ijerph10010417

James, P., Hart, J. E., Banay, R. F., & Laden, F. (2016). Exposure to greenness and mortality in a nationwide prospective cohort study of women. *Environmental Health Perspectives*, *124*(9), 1344–1352. https://doi.org/10.1289/ehp.1510363

Jensen, F. S., & Koch, N. E. (2004). Twenty-five years of forest recreation research in Denmark and its influence on forest policy. *Scandinavian Journal of Forest Research*, *19*(S4), 93–102.

Kaspar, H. (2012). *Erlebnis Stadtpark: Nutzung und Wahrnehmung urbaner Grünräume*. Springer-Verlag.

Kearney, A. R. (2006). Residential development patterns and neighborhood satisfaction. *Environment and Behavior*, *38*(1), 112–139. https://doi.org/10.1177/0013916505277607

Kemperman, A., & Timmermans, H. (2014). Green spaces in the direct living environment and social contacts of the aging population. *Landscape and Urban Planning*, *129*, 44–54. https://doi.org/10.1016/j.landurbplan.2014.05.003

Kölner Statistische Nachrichten. (2023). *Statistisches Jahrbuch 2022 –* Stadtgebiet und Flächennutzung. Report No. 9. https://www.stadt-koeln.de/mediaasset/content/pdf15/statistik-jahrbuch/jahrbuchkapitel_0_stadtgebiet_und_fl%C3%B5chennutzung_2022.pdf.

Krekel, C., Kolbe, J., & Wüstemann, H. (2016). The greener, the happier? The effect of urban land use on residential well-being. *Ecological Economics*, *121*, 117–127. https://doi.org/10.1016/j.ecolecon.2015.11.005

Kweon, B.-S., Ellis, C., Leiva, P., & Rogers, G. (2010). Landscape components, land use, and neighborhood satisfaction. *Environment and Planning B: Planning and Design*, *37*, 500–517. https://doi.org/10.1068/b35059

Łaszkiewicz, E., Kronenberg, J., Mohamed, A. A., Roitsch, D., & De Vreese, R. (2023). Who does not use urban green spaces and why? Insights from a comparative study of thirty-three European countries. *Landscape and Urban Planning*, *239*, 104866. https://doi.org/10.1016/j.landurbplan.2023.104866

Lee, S. M., Conway, T. L., Frank, L. D., Saelens, B. E., Cain, K. L., & Sallis, J. F. (2016). The relation of perceived and objective environment attributes to neighborhood satisfaction. *Environment and Behavior*, *49*(2), 136–160. https://doi.org/10.1177/0013916515623823

Lovasi, G. S., Schwartz-Soicher, O., Quinn, J. W., Berger, D. K., Neckerman, K. M., Jaslow, R., Lee, K. K., & Rundle, A. (2013). Neighborhood safety and green space as predictors of obesity among preschool children from low-income families in New York City. *Preventive Medicine*, *57*(3), 189–193. https://doi.org/10.1016/j.ypmed.2013.05.012

Maas, J., van Dillen, S. M. E., Verheij, R. A., & Groenewegen, P. P. (2009). Social contacts as a possible mechanism behind the relation between green space and health. *Health & Place*, *15*(2), 586–595. https://doi.org/10.1016/j.healthplace.2008.09.006

Mak, B. K. L., & Jim, C. Y. (2019). Linking park users' socio-demographic characteristics and visit-related preferences to improve urban parks. *Cities*, *92*, 97–111. https://doi.org/10.1016/j.cities.2019.03.008

Pinto, L., Ferreira, C. S. S., & Pereira, P. (2021). Environmental and socioeconomic factors influencing the use of urban green spaces in

Coimbra (Portugal). *Science of the Total Environment*, *792*, 148293. https://doi.org/10.1016/j.scitotenv.2021.148293

Schebella, M. F., Weber, D., Schultz, L., & Weinstein, P. (2019). The wellbeing benefits associated with perceived and measured biodiversity in Australian urban green spaces. *Sustainability*, *11*(3). https://doi.org/10.3390/su11030802

Statistisches Amt für Hamburg und Schleswig-Holstein. (2021). *Bodenflächen in Hamburg am 31.12. 2020 nach Art der tatsächlichen Nutzung*. Report No. AV1-j20HH. https://www.statistik-nord.de/fileadmin/Dokumente/Statistische_Berichte/andere_statistiken/A_V_1_H_gebiet_flaeche/A_V_1_j20_HH.pdf

Tinsley, H. E., Tinsley, D. J., & Croskeys, C. E. (2002). Park usage, social milieu, and psychosocial benefits of park use reported by older urban park users from four ethnic groups. *Leisure Sciences*, *24*(2), 199–218. https://doi.org/10.1080/01490400252900158

van den Berg, A. E., Maas, J., Verheij, R. A., & Groenewegen, P. P. (2010). Green space as a buffer between stressful life events and health. *Social Science & Medicine*, *70*(8), 1203–1210. https://doi.org/10.1016/j.socscimed.2010.01.002

Wang, R., Feng, Z., & Pearce, J. (2022). Neighbourhood greenspace quantity, quality and socioeconomic inequalities in mental health. *Cities*, *129*. https://doi.org/10.1016/j.cities.2022.103815

Wei, D., Lu, Y., Wu, X., Ho, H. C., Wu, W., Song, J., & Wang, Y. (2023). Greenspace exposure may increase life expectancy of elderly adults, especially for those with low socioeconomic status. *Health & Place*, *84*, 103142. https://doi.org/10.1016/j.healthplace.2023.103142

Weng, M., Ding, N., Li, J., Jin, X., Xiao, H., He, Z., & Su, S. (2019). The 15-minute walkable neighborhoods: Measurement, social inequalities and implications for building healthy communities in urban China. *Journal of Transport & Health*, *13*, 259–273. https://doi.org/10.1016/j.jth.2019.05.005

White, M., Smith, A., Humphryes, K., Pahl, S., Snelling, D., & Depledge, M. (2010). Blue space: The importance of water for preference, affect, and restorativeness ratings of natural and built scenes. *Journal of Environmental Psychology*, *30*(4), 482–493. https://doi.org/10.1016/j.jenvp.2010.04.004

White, M. P., Alcock, I., Wheeler, B. W., & Depledge, M. H. (2013). Would you be happier living in a greener urban area? A fixed-effects analysis of panel data. *Psychological Science*, *24*(6), 920–928. https://doi.org/10.1177/0956797612464659

Willsher, K. (2020). Paris mayor unveils '15-minute city' plan in re-election campaign. *The Guardian*. www.theguardian.com/world/2020/feb/07/paris-mayor-unveils-15-minute-city-plan-in-re-election-campaign

Wu, W., Dong, G., Sun, Y., & Yun, Y. (2020). Contextualized effects of park access and usage on residential satisfaction: A spatial approach. *Land Use Policy*, *94*. https://doi.org/10.1016/j.landusepol.2020.104532

Zhang, Y., van den Berg, A. E., Van Dijk, T., & Weitkamp, G. (2017). Quality over quantity: Contribution of urban green space to neighborhood satisfaction. *International Journal of Environmental Research and Public Health*, *14*(5), 535. https://doi.org/10.3390/ijerph14050535

4 Nature relatedness in cities

As discussed in Chapter 1, biophilia theory (Kellert & Wilson, 1993) suggests that individuals living in cities, in particular, might instinctively seek proximity to natural experiences due to evolutionary development and the relatively recent emergence of urban environments. At the same time, cultural development suggests that some individuals prefer a combination of natural and urban surroundings (Joye & De Block, 2011; Joye & van den Berg, 2011), especially when attractive urban settings are perceived as scenic or beautiful, similar to natural environments (Seresinhe et al., 2019). Urban dwellers' nature relatedness may influence both their decision to live in more or less green areas and their use of available nature facilities. Therefore, it is crucial to consider the degree of urban residents' need for nature, specifically their nature relatedness, when analysing the importance of green spaces in cities for well-being and its multiple aspects.

Several studies analysing connectedness to nature and its impact on well-being highlight the importance of this individual disposition as a predictor of subjective well-being (Capaldi et al., 2014; Cervinka et al., 2012; Howell et al., 2011; Martin et al., 2020; Mayer & Frantz, 2004; Nisbet & Zelenski, 2020; Nisbet et al., 2011; Pritchard et al., 2019; Zelenski & Nisbet, 2014). While feeling connected in general, whether to friends or one's country, is associated with happiness and well-being, the unique impact of connectedness to nature on happiness remains even when other types of general connectedness are taken into account (Zelenski & Nisbet, 2014). However, understanding the precise mechanisms linking nature connectedness, general individual connectedness, mindfulness, meaning in life, and overall well-being is still the subject of research (cf. Howell et al., 2011; Zelenski & Nisbet, 2014). Nonetheless, several meta-analyses (Barragan-Jason et al., 2023; Capaldi et al., 2014; Pritchard et al., 2019) that have examined the relationship between nature connectedness and happiness highlight that individuals with a stronger affinity to nature appear to report higher levels of happiness and greater overall life satisfaction.

Beyond the direct link between nature connectedness and well-being, it is interesting to see how an individual's nature relatedness might influence the

DOI: 10.4324/9781003546146-5

impact of green spaces on well-being. However, there are not many studies that examine whether a person's nature relatedness modifies this association in any way. For instance, Chang et al. (2020) demonstrated that people with high nature relatedness experienced a significant increase in life satisfaction when using green spaces, in contrast to those with low nature relatedness. Similarly, McMahan et al. (2018) demonstrated a moderating effect of closeness to nature in an experiment with lab-based natural and built environments, with individuals who were more connected to nature showing higher levels of emotional well-being. At the same time, Martin et al. (2020) found that people with low levels of nature connectedness tended to experience higher levels of happiness through more frequent visits to green spaces, while such visits no longer have a significant effect on well-being for people with high levels of nature connectedness. To understand how nature connectedness acts as a mediator in the relationship between exposure to nature and effects on well-being, Mayer et al. (2009) conducted an experimental study and found that spending time in nature strengthens nature connectedness, which leads to increased feelings of happiness.

Although the direction of influence and the role of nature connectedness in the mechanisms linking green space components to well-being are not entirely clear in these studies, it seems clear that personal closeness to nature is important. In particular, nature relatedness appears to act as a variable that influences this complex relationship, and affects how green spaces influence well-being. This personal trait plays an important role in how people use nature, choose greener residential areas, and experience the impact on well-being.

Measurement and methodological considerations

Measuring nature relatedness is about capturing respondents' attitudes and behaviours towards nature, and their perception of nature as something worth protecting. The three most commonly used scales for measuring nature relatedness, listed later, originate from different theoretical approaches, while the operationalisation of the construct is mostly based on its three interrelated components. The first component, the affective or emotional aspect, examines a person's feelings towards nature. The second component, the cognitive or mental aspect, relates to how the individual personally perceives the importance of nature, and why it is important to protect it. The third component, the conative or action-orientated aspect, focuses on the behaviours a person adopts as a result of their affinity with nature.

The New Environmental Paradigm (NEP) scale (Dunlap et al., 2000) provides an approach to measuring nature relatedness that focuses mainly on the cognitive and conative dimensions. The revised scale consists of 15 items (whereas the original scale contained 12 items), ranging from *strongly agree* to *strongly disagree*. While the overall validity of the NEP scale has been widely tested, there have been conflicting study results as to whether the scale measures a single construct or is multidimensional (Dunlap et al., 2000).

The Connectedness to Nature Scale (CNS) (Mayer & Frantz, 2004; Mayer et al., 2009) measures both affective and cognitive components of nature relatedness, excluding behavioural aspects. It consists of 14 items on a response scale ranging from *strongly disagree* to *strongly agree*, and is primarily designed to measure individuals' perception of themselves as part of the natural world, their connection to animals and plants, and their sense of equality between themselves and nature. Several studies have confirmed the reliability and validity of the CNS scale, in which items load on a single factor and have high internal consistency (Mayer & Frantz, 2004).

Nisbet et al. (2009, 2011) use the nature relatedness (NR) scale to assess the affective (self), cognitive (perspective), and conative (experience) components of nature relatedness. The validity of the scale was assessed using 21 items belonging to each of these three components. Similar to previous scales, participants were asked to rate the items on a Likert scale ranging from *strongly disagree* to *strongly agree*.

Studies analysing the relationship among these three commonly used measurement scales show a high correlation between the CNS and NEP scales. However, when lifestyle or behavioural measures are included in the analysis, the CNS and NEP scales may be measuring different constructs (Mayer & Frantz, 2004). Additionally, the NEP scale shows a strong correlation with the NR scale (Nisbet et al., 2009), or at least with some of its components (Nisbet et al., 2011).

As the focus of the current study is on well-being outcomes (and originally on relocation behaviour), it was important to use a scale that captures all three aspects of nature relatedness: emotional, behavioural, and action-orientated components. Therefore, the NR scale developed by Nisbet et al. (2009, 2011) was selected. The questionnaire used a reduced version of this scale, excluding items with comparatively low factor loadings in the original study by Nisbet et al. (2009). Consequently, the questionnaire included the three items with the highest factor loadings for each of the three components of nature relatedness (items 1–9 in Table 4.1).

Several authors emphasise the role of childhood nature experiences in shaping perceptions of the natural environment in adulthood. A consistent aspect of their findings is the positive correlation between increased exposure to nature in childhood and a higher likelihood of maintaining such a connection to nature in adulthood (Rosa et al., 2018). Thompson et al. (2008) demonstrate that visits to nature in childhood increase the likelihood of visiting green spaces alone as an adult, while a lack of such visits in childhood is linked to fewer visits to green spaces in adulthood. Additionally, the amount of outdoor physical activity with parents in childhood shows a positive association with the degree of nature relatedness in adulthood (Puhakka et al., 2018). Moreover, individuals who grew up in houses with gardens are more likely

Table 4.1 Measurement of nature relatedness, based on Nisbet et al. (2009)

Component	*Item*	*Mean*	*Factor 1*
Affective (self)	My connection to nature and the environment is a part of my spirituality	4.15	0.67
	My relationship to nature is an important part of who I am	5.18	0.79
	I feel very connected to all living things and the earth	5.04	0.71
Cognitive (perspective)	Humans have the right to use natural resources any way we want (reversed)	5.22	0.08
	Conservation is unnecessary because nature is strong enough to recover from any human impact (reversed)	6.41	0.15
	Animals, birds, and plants have fewer rights than humans (reversed)	5.48	0.23
Conative (experience)	The thought of being deep in the woods, away from civilisation, is frightening	4.96	0.34
	My ideal vacation spot would be a remote, wilder-ness area	4.39	0.55
	I enjoy being outdoors, even in unpleasant weather	4.34	0.56
Childhood and parenting	I have many pleasant memories of trips to nature as a child	5.47	0.49
	As raising children, it is or it would be important to me to give my child an understanding of nature	6.23	0.59

Notes: Survey data from Hamburg and Cologne, collected in 2020/2021 (N = 1840); means (on scale 1–7) design weighted. Factor 1 eigenvalue > 2.9 explains most of the variance in the data (factor 2 eigenvalue < 0.53).

to choose residential areas with similar green spaces in adulthood (Kley & Stenpaß, 2020). In the present study, therefore, it was decided to extend the nature relatedness scale by adding two additional items about respondents' childhood experiences, and the importance of proximity to nature in their own parenting practices. The wording of these items (items 10–11) was adapted from the study on nature awareness commissioned by the German Federal Agency for Nature Conservation[1] (Kleinhückelkotten & Neitzke, 2010).

For the items on the nature relatedness scale shown in Table 4.1, respondents were asked to rate them on a seven-point Likert scale from *strongly disagree* to *strongly agree*. The choice of a seven-point scale was made to fit the general format of the survey, and to ensure consistency with other questions (cf. Franzen, 2019). The overall sample showed good reliability of the 11-item scale with an alpha value of 0.74. In order to ensure the unidimensionality of the scale, a factor analysis was conducted in which three items were reversed (items 4–6). The eigenvalues indicated that a single-factor solution was the most suitable. The single-factor solution with an eigenvalue of 2.9 explained

94% of the variance. All items loaded positively on the first factor, with an average factor loading of 0.47. The subsequent factor, with an eigenvalue of 0.53, explained only 17% of the variance and would include only four items (items 4–7) with loadings above 0.1. The mean value of the nature relatedness scale is 5.24, with a standard deviation of 0.92.

Nature relatedness in life course phases and social classes

While studies on differences in attitudes and lifestyles towards nature are more common (cf. Hedlund-de Witt et al., 2014; Nisbet et al., 2009), studies reporting differences or similarities in nature relatedness across different life course phases or social classes are rare. Cervinka et al. (2012) found no significant differences in nature relatedness across respondents' levels of education but observed variations in nature connectedness according to age, demonstrating that older respondents tend to be more connected to nature than younger respondents. Women were also found to be more nature related than men (Cervinka et al., 2012; Rosa et al., 2018). As Chapter 3 demonstrated distinctions in the frequency and motives for using green spaces across different life course phases and social classes, it is reasonable to assume that nature relatedness might also vary across the life course and social classes.

The average levels of nature relatedness in the young adult, family, midlife, and senior life course phases are shown in Figure 4.1. The young adult phase has the lowest level of nature relatedness at 4.9, significantly lower than the other three life course phases, which is consistent with previous research (Cervinka et al., 2012). The subsequent life course phases demonstrate similar levels

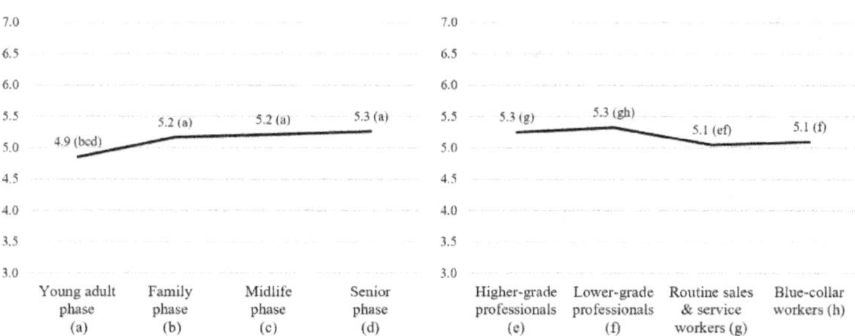

Figure 4.1 Nature relatedness by life course phase (left) and social class (right)

Notes: Estimates design weighted; survey data from Hamburg and Cologne, collected in 2020/2021. Young adult phase (N = 169), family phase (N = 240), midlife phase (N = 994), and senior phase (N = 437). Higher-grade professionals (N = 296), lower-grade professionals (N = 618), routine sales and service workers (N = 600), and blue-collar workers (N = 326).

(a/b/c/d) significant difference ($p < 0.05$) between life course phases.

(e/f/g/h) significant difference ($p < 0.05$) between social classes.

of nature relatedness, while the senior phase shows a slight, non-significant increase in nature relatedness compared to the previous two phases (5.3 and 5.2, respectively). This suggests that the nature relatedness tends to increase over the life course, with the strongest increase occurring during the transition to the family or midlife phase, followed by a marginal increase thereafter.

As far as the variations across social classes are concerned (Figure 4.1, right), nature relatedness is slightly stronger in the higher social classes of professionals than in the lower classes. Both classes of professionals have an average nature relatedness score of 5.3. In contrast, blue-collar workers, and routine sales and service workers have a slightly lower nature relatedness of 5.1. The lowest level of nature relatedness is found among routine sales and service workers, which is significantly lower compared to the two higher classes of professionals.

One possible reason for these class differences could be access to and use of green spaces, as contact with nature seems to increase connectedness with it (Mayer et al., 2009). As we have seen in Figure 3.3, the results suggest that higher social classes use nature in the neighbourhood more frequently, at least on a weekly basis, and Figure 3.4 shows that they are also more likely to have their own gardens. The small difference between the two lower social classes, which is not quite apparent in the rounded figures in Figure 4.1, where blue-collar workers are slightly more likely to be nature related than routine sales and service workers, may be due to the fact that blue-collar workers spend more time on typical activities in green spaces in the neighbourhood, as shown in Figure 3.16.

Note

1 A representative survey conducted every two years by the Federal Ministry for the Environment, Nature Conservation, Nuclear Safety and Consumer Protection, along with the Federal Agency for Nature Conservation.

References

Barragan-Jason, G., Loreau, M., de Mazancourt, C., Singer, M. C., & Parmesan, C. (2023). Psychological and physical connections with nature improve both human well-being and nature conservation: A systematic review of meta-analyses. *Biological Conservation*, *277*, 109842. https://doi.org/10.1016/j.biocon.2022.109842

Capaldi, C. A., Dopko, R. L., & Zelenski, J. M. (2014). The relationship between nature connectedness and happiness: A meta-analysis. *Frontiers in Psychology*, *5*, 976. https://doi.org/10.3389/fpsyg.2014.00976

Cervinka, R., Röderer, K., & Hefler, E. (2012). Are nature lovers happy? On various indicators of well-being and connectedness with nature. *Journal of Health Psychology*, *17*(3), 379–388. https://doi.org/10.1177/1359105311416873

Chang, C.-C., Oh, R. R. Y., Nghiem, T. P. L., Zhang, Y., Tan, C. L. Y., Lin, B. B., Gaston, K. J., Fuller, R. A., & Carrasco, L. R. (2020). Life satisfaction linked to the diversity of nature experiences and nature views from the window. *Landscape and Urban Planning*, *202*, 103874. https://doi.org/10.1016/j.landurbplan.2020.103874

Dunlap, R. E., Van Liere, K. D., Mertig, A. G., & Jones, R. E. (2000). New trends in measuring environmental attitudes: Measuring endorsement of the new ecological paradigm: A revised NEP scale. *Journal of Social Issues*, *56*(3), 425–442. https://doi.org/10.1111/0022-4537.00176

Franzen, A. (2019). Antwortskalen in standardisierten Befragungen. *Handbuch Methoden der empirischen Sozialforschung*, 843–854.

Hedlund-de Witt, A., de Boer, J., & Boersema, J. J. (2014). Exploring inner and outer worlds: A quantitative study of worldviews, environmental attitudes, and sustainable lifestyles. *Journal of Environmental Psychology*, *37*, 40–54. https://doi.org/10.1016/j.jenvp.2013.11.005

Howell, A. J., Dopko, R. L., Passmore, H.-A., & Buro, K. (2011). Nature connectedness: Associations with well-being and mindfulness. *Personality and Individual Differences*, *51*(2), 166–171. https://doi.org/10.1016/j.paid.2011.03.037

Joye, Y., & De Block, A. (2011). 'Nature and I are two': A critical examination of the biophilia hypothesis. *Environmental Values*, *20*(2), 189–215. https://doi.org/10.3197/096327111x12997574391724

Joye, Y., & van den Berg, A. (2011). Is love for green in our genes? A critical analysis of evolutionary assumptions in restorative environments research. *Urban Forestry & Urban Greening*, *10*(4), 261–268. https://doi.org/10.1016/j.ufug.2011.07.004

Kellert, S., & Wilson, E. (1993). *The biophilia hypothesis*. Island Press.

Kleinhückelkotten, S., & Neitzke, H. P. (2010). Umfrage Naturbewusstsein. *Abschlussbericht*. ECOLOG-Institut, Hannover.

Kley, S., & Stenpaß, A. (2020). Intergenerational transmission of housing choice: The relevance of green spaces for moving into a family house across social class. *Population, Space and Place*, *26*(2), 2299. https://doi.org/10.1002/psp.2299

Martin, L., White, M. P., Hunt, A., Richardson, M., Pahl, S., & Burt, J. (2020). Nature contact, nature connectedness and associations with health, wellbeing and pro-environmental behaviours. *Journal of Environmental Psychology*, *68*, 101389. https://doi.org/10.1016/j.jenvp.2020.101389

Mayer, F. S., & Frantz, C. M. (2004). The connectedness to nature scale: A measure of individuals' feeling in community with nature. *Journal of Environmental Psychology*, *24*(4), 503–515. https://doi.org/10.1016/j.jenvp.2004.10.001

Mayer, F. S., McPherson Franz, C., & Bruehlman-Senecal, E. (2009). Why is nature beneficial? The role of connectedness to nature. *Environment and Behavior*, *41*(5), 607–643. https://doi.org/10.1177/0013916508319745

McMahan, E. A., Estes, D., Murfin, J. S., & Bryan, C. M. (2018). Nature connectedness moderates the effect of nature exposure on explicit and implicit measures of emotion. *Journal of Positive Psychology and Wellbeing*, *2*(2), 128–148.

Nisbet, E. K., & Zelenski, J. M. (2020). Nature relatedness and subjective well-being. In F. Maggino (Ed.), *Encyclopedia of quality of life and well-being research* (pp. 1–9). Springer International Publishing. https://doi.org/10.1007/978-3-319-69909-7_3909-2

Nisbet, E. K., Zelenski, J. M., & Murphy, S. A. (2009). The nature relatedness scale. *Environment and Behavior*, *41*(5), 715–740. https://doi.org/10.1177/0013916508318748

Nisbet, E. K., Zelenski, J. M., & Murphy, S. A. (2011). Happiness is in our nature: Exploring nature relatedness as a contributor to subjective well-being. *Journal of Happiness Studies*, *12*(2), 303–322. https://doi.org/10.1007/s10902-010-9197-7

Pritchard, A., Richardson, M., Sheffield, D., & McEwan, K. (2019). The relationship between nature connectedness and eudaimonic well-being: A meta-analysis. *Journal of Happiness Studies*, *21*(3), 1145–1167. https://doi.org/10.1007/s10902-019-00118-6

Puhakka, S., Pyky, R., Lankila, T., Kangas, M., Rusanen, J., Ikäheimo, T. M., Koivumaa-Honkanen, H., & Korpelainen, R. (2018). Physical activity, residential environment, and nature relatedness in young men – a population-based MOPO study. *International Journal of Environmental Research and Public Health*, *15*(10), 2322. https://doi.org/10.3390/ijerph15102322

Rosa, C. D., Profice, C. C., & Collado, S. (2018). Nature experiences and adults' self-reported pro-environmental behaviors: The role of connectedness to nature and childhood nature experiences. *Frontiers in Psychology*, *9*, 1055. https://doi.org/10.3389/fpsyg.2018.01055

Seresinhe, C. I., Preis, T., Mackerron, G., & Moat, H. S. (2019). Happiness is greater in more scenic locations. *Scientific Reports*, *9*(1). https://doi.org/10.1038/s41598-019-40854-6

Thompson, C. W., Aspinall, P., & Montarzino, A. (2008). The childhood factor: Adult visits to green places and the significance of childhood experience. *Environment and Behavior*, *40*(1), 111–143. https://doi.org/10.1177/0013916507300119

Zelenski, J. M., & Nisbet, E. K. (2014). Happiness and feeling connected: The distinct role of nature relatedness. *Environment and Behavior*, *46*(1), 3–23. https://doi.org/10.1177/0013916512451901

5 Satisfaction with green spaces in the neighbourhood

Despite the extensive research on the effects of green spaces on health, well-being, and residential satisfaction outlined in Chapter 1, comparatively few attempts have been made to identify the specific factors that influence satisfaction with green spaces in urban areas, especially with regard to different life course phases or socio-economic classes.

While satisfaction with green spaces is often used as a predictor to explain health outcomes (Liu et al., 2019; Qiao et al., 2021; Ruijsbroek et al., 2017), subjective well-being (McEachan et al., 2018; Zhao et al., 2024), residential satisfaction (Permentier et al., 2010), and relocation processes (Dovbischuk & Kley, 2024), only a few studies have considered satisfaction with neighbourhood green spaces as an outcome variable (Kearney, 2006; Qiao et al., 2021; Wu et al., 2019). As expected, factors such as the number of green spaces (Qiao et al., 2021), distance to parks (Wu et al., 2019), and proximity to other larger natural areas (Kearney, 2006) seem to influence satisfaction with neighbourhood green spaces. However, the specific types of green spaces that influence satisfaction with nature in urban areas, or differences across life course phases and social classes, remain largely unknown.

As shown earlier in Figure 3.5, satisfaction with nature varies across both life course phases and social classes. In terms of life course differences, studies have found significant differences in nature satisfaction according to age (Qiao et al., 2021; Wu et al., 2019) and the presence of children (Kearney, 2006). In terms of social class, research suggests that education and income levels have a significant impact on satisfaction with neighbourhood green spaces, with higher income and education levels correlating with higher satisfaction (Wu et al., 2019).

This chapter analyses satisfaction with neighbourhood green spaces, taking into account relevant predictors in different life course phases and social classes. Previous research has highlighted the relevance of green space availability for satisfaction with green spaces (Kearney, 2006; Qiao et al., 2021; Wu et al., 2019). Therefore, the following regression models in Table 5.1 and 5.2 include the availability of different types of green spaces in the neighbourhood, such as parks, waterfront areas, woods, and fields. These different types

DOI: 10.4324/9781003546146-6

of green spaces might vary in their relevance for nature satisfaction in certain life course phases or social classes.

Additionally, the models take into account whether respondents have access to private or shared green spaces, as this could influence their satisfaction (Kley & Dovbischuk, 2021, 2024; Zhao et al., 2024). Furthermore, respondents' nature relatedness is considered (Nisbet et al., 2009), as this could potentially influence the relevance of green spaces for nature satisfaction, similar to other satisfaction sub-domains (Chang et al., 2020; Martin et al., 2020; McMahan et al., 2018). Moreover, it may be relevant whether individuals regularly visit natural amenities outside their neighbourhood, as this could influence their use behaviour of green spaces in the neighbourhood.

As discussed in Chapter 2, Hamburg is a much greener city compared to Cologne (Tröger et al., 2016). Therefore, it is important to include respondents' city of residence in the models, as it is plausible that nature satisfaction could be higher in Hamburg. Additionally, age (Qiao et al., 2021; Wu et al., 2019) and gender might be important predictors of nature satisfaction, as women seem to have higher levels of nature relatedness (Cervinka et al., 2012; Rosa et al., 2018). Income could be another important predictor (Wu et al., 2019), as wealthier respondents might reside in areas with more green spaces (Wolch et al., 2005, 2014). For household characteristics, single occupancy is controlled for, as singles might use neighbourhood green spaces differently than non-singles. Homeownership is considered as a control variable, as it could influence both residential choice (Clark & Huang, 2003; Coulter, 2013; Dovbischuk & Kley, 2024; Kley, 2011) and satisfaction levels (Kley & Dovbischuk, 2024; Permentier et al., 2010).

As the level of neighbourhood safety (Wu et al., 2019) and the density of important life points (Qiao et al., 2021) have been found to influence satisfaction with green spaces, it is important to consider objective characteristics of the neighbourhood. Therefore, the neighbourhood reputation variable is included in the models. Research suggests that this variable effectively reflects the objective characteristics of a residential area, such as the crime rate, the availability of services, and the wealth status of the neighbourhood (Permentier et al., 2010). Additionally, the models take into account proximity to the city centre based on the respondents' city districts.

To account for the potential negative influence of the COVID-19 pandemic, its impact is also included in the analysis. As the study was conducted after the outbreak of the pandemic, respondents' perceptions of neighbourhood green spaces may have been affected (Berdejo-Espinola et al., 2021). The COVID-19 negative impact index, which ranges from 0 to 4, reflects whether respondents experienced financial difficulties, reduced participation in hobbies, spatial confinement at home or less time for physical activity as a result of the COVID-19 pandemic.

As the study covered the period from September to February, it is important to consider the seasons. Although it has been shown that there is little difference in the use of urban green spaces across seasons (Lachowycz et al., 2012; Mak & Jim, 2019), this could potentially affect satisfaction with nature. Additionally, the models consider the average number of hours of sunshine on the day of the survey, as this could also influence individual responses regarding satisfaction with neighbourhood nature.

Nature satisfaction in life course phases and social classes

Across all life course phases and social classes (see Table 5.1 for life course phases and Table 5.2 for social classes), *parks* prove to be the most important factor influencing the nature satisfaction of city dwellers in the young adult

Table 5.1 Satisfaction with neighbourhood green spaces[6] regressed on the availability of green spaces, by life course phase

	Young adult phase (AME)	*Family phase (AME)*	*Midlife phase (AME)*	*Senior phase (AME)*
Parks available	0.72*	0.28	−0.10	0.17
Waterfronts available	0.37	−0.14	0.42***	0.49***
Woods available	0.23	0.19	0.53***	0.13
Fields available	0.66**	0.21	0.07	0.05
Hamburg (ref.: Cologne)	0.11	0.16	0.20*	0.21+
Female	−0.08	0.21	0.09	0.25*
Age	−0.06*	0.00	0.00	0.00
Income, in tsd. EUR[1]	0.12	0.17+	0.04	0.08
One-person household	0.37+	0.28	−0.11	0.10
Homeownership	0.56+	0.44*	0.10	0.02
Duration of residence, in years	0.01	−0.01	0.01**	0.00
Own garden	0.19	−0.01	0.23*	0.26
Own balcony	0.12	0.36+	0.21*	0.04
Shared yard	−0.06	0.50*	−0.22*	−0.19
Nature relatedness	0.07	0.09	0.17**	0.11
COVID-19 negative effects[2]	0.10	−0.02	−0.09*	−0.09
Nature beyond neighbourhood[3]	−0.33	0.45*	0.19+	0.18
Neighbourhood reputation[4]	0.10	0.39**	0.30***	0.33**

(*Continued*)

Table 5.1 (Continued)

	Young adult phase (AME)	*Family phase (AME)*	*Midlife phase (AME)*	*Senior phase (AME)*
Central district	–0.19	–0.06	–0.27*	–0.30*
Survey in winter	–0.58*	–0.22	–0.11	–0.19
Sunshine hours/ survey day[5]	0.04	0.01	–0.01	–0.01
No. of persons	169	240	994	437
R2 (degrees of freedom)	0.408 (22)	0.254 (22)	0.276 (22)	0.199 (22)

Notes: Ordinary least squares (OLS) regression, design weighted, robust standard errors applied.

$+p < 0.1$, $*\ p < 0.05$, $**\ p < 0.01$, $***\ p < 0.001$.

1 Equivalised according to OECD standards (OECD, n.d.): monthly household income divided by the square root of household members (i.e. weighted household size), with partial imputation of respondents' income.

2 Index (0/4) assessing financial hardship, less participation in hobbies, spatial confinement feelings at home, and reduced time for physical activity due to the COVID-19 pandemic.

3 Nature amenities that are further than a 15-minute walk from home, and are used at least several times a month.

4 Measured on a scale from 1 (very bad) to 4 (very good).

5 The data on average sunshine hours on the respective survey days were retrospectively matched with the survey data. Sunshine data were obtained from the weather stations at Hamburg Airport and Cologne Airport (data from WetterKontor GmbH).

6 Measured on a scale of 1–7 with the question 'How satisfied are you with the availability of nature in your neighbourhood?'.

phase. *Waterfronts* remain important for neighbourhood nature satisfaction across all social classes, albeit with varying effect sizes. Regarding the life course phases, waterfronts have no significant influence on nature satisfaction in the young adult and family phases. Among the social classes, lower-grade professionals are the only group for whom *woods* have no effect on nature satisfaction. As far as the life course phases are concerned, woods are particularly relevant in the midlife phase. In the case of *fields*, their availability plays an important role in nature satisfaction in the young adult phase. In terms of social classes, fields are not relevant for the highest and lowest social classes, but they are important for both the middle social classes of lower-grade professionals and routine sales and service workers.

The relevance of private or shared green spaces also varies across life course phases and social classes. Private or shared green spaces are irrelevant for nature satisfaction in the more affluent social classes or in the young adult and senior phases. In fact, the presence of a shared green yard (which presumably means living in a block of flats) appears to diminish satisfaction with neighbourhood green spaces among routine sales and service workers,

Table 5.2 Satisfaction with neighbourhood green spaces[1] regressed on the availability of green spaces, by social class

	Higher-grade professionals (AME)	*Lower-grade professionals (AME)*	*Routine sales and service workers (AME)*	*Blue-collar workers (AME)*
Parks available	0.03	0.07	0.18	0.07
Waterfronts available	0.36*	0.26*	0.45***	0.33+
Woods available	0.58***	0.19	0.45*	0.46*
Fields available	–0.16	0.36**	0.30*	–0.12
Hamburg (ref.: Cologne)	0.10	0.36*	0.15	0.19
Female	0.21	0.29*	0.04	–0.08
Age	0.01	0.00	0.01	–0.01
Income, in tsd. EUR[1]	0.07	0.06	–0.07	–0.01
One-person household	–0.03	–0.06	–0.17	–0.15
Homeownership	0.27	0.16	0.24+	0.08
Duration of residence, in years	0.00	0.01	0.01	0.01*
Own garden	0.04	0.18	0.11	0.57**
Own balcony	0.16	0.13	0.17	0.20
Shared yard	–0.20	–0.09	–0.24 +	–0.12
Nature relatedness	0.09	0.10	0.16 *	0.31**
COVID-19 negative effects[1]	–0.20*	–0.10*	0.04	–0.03
Nature beyond neighbourhood[1]	0.21	0.09	0.00	0.41 *
Neighbourhood reputation[1]	0.27*	0.37***	0.31**	0.20
Central district	–0.17	–0.32*	–0.22	–0.27
Survey in winter	–0.07	–0.08	–0.24+	–0.52**
Sunshine hours/ survey day[1]	0.04	–0.02	0.01	–0.04
No. of persons	296	618	600	326
R2 (degrees of freedom)	0.238 (22)	0.260 (22)	0.246 (22)	0.279 (22)

Notes: OLS regression, design weighted, robust standard errors applied.
+ $p < 0.1$, * $p < 0.05$, ** $p < 0.01$, *** $p < 0.001$.
[1] See Table 5.1.

and individuals in the midlife phase. For the latter group, however, having a private balcony or garden increases their satisfaction with nature. Access to private balconies or shared green yards also enhances satisfaction with local nature in the family phase. Private gardens and visiting nature outside the immediate neighbourhood seem to be particularly important for nature satisfaction among people in the lowest social class of blue-collar workers.

Additionally, in the family and midlife phases, exploring nature elsewhere strengthens satisfaction with local nature. Furthermore, nature relatedness additionally increases nature satisfaction, particularly in the midlife phase and for individuals in the two lower social classes.

The importance of the city of residence is particularly evident in the later life course stages of midlife and senior phases, or among lower-grade professionals. Age only plays a role in the young adult phase, where older individuals are less satisfied with the nature of their neighbourhood. Women tend to be more satisfied with neighbourhood nature in the senior phase and among lower-grade professionals. Household income plays a minor role, except in the family phase. In terms of household characteristics, single households in the young adult phase tend to be more satisfied with neighbourhood nature. Additionally, homeownership emerges as an important factor increasing nature satisfaction in the young adult and family phases, as well as among routine sales and service workers.

Neighbourhood reputation, which reflects the objective qualities of the residential environment, proves to be important in most life course phases and social classes: exceptions are the young adult phase and the lowest social class of blue-collar workers, where satisfaction with nature is largely unaffected by other objective neighbourhood characteristics. Living close to the city centre has a negative effect on nature satisfaction in all groups, with a significantly stronger effect in the lower-grade professionals and in the later life course stages of midlife and senior phases.

The negative impact of the pandemic lowers satisfaction with nature in the neighbourhood in the more affluent social classes of professionals and in the midlife phase. Additionally, the colder winter season has a negative effect on nature satisfaction in all subgroups, although this effect is only significant in the young adult phase and in the lower social classes. The presence of sunny weather on the day of the survey does not appear to have a significant effect on satisfaction with nature in the neighbourhood.

References

Berdejo-Espinola, V., Suárez-Castro, A. F., Amano, T., Fielding, K. S., Oh, R. R. Y., & Fuller, R. A. (2021). Urban green space use during a time of stress: A case study during the COVID-19 pandemic in Brisbane, Australia. *People and Nature*, *3*(3), 597–609. https://doi.org/10.1002/pan3.10218

Cervinka, R., Röderer, K., & Hefler, E. (2012). Are nature lovers happy? On various indicators of well-being and connectedness with nature. *Journal of Health Psychology*, *17*(3), 379–388. https://doi.org/10.1177/1359105311416873

Chang, C.-C., Oh, R. R. Y., Nghiem, T. P. L., Zhang, Y., Tan, C. L. Y., Lin, B. B., Gaston, K. J., Fuller, R. A., & Carrasco, L. R. (2020). Life satisfaction linked to the diversity of nature experiences and nature views from the window. *Landscape and Urban Planning*, *202*, 103874. https://doi.org/10.1016/j.landurbplan.2020.103874

Clark, W. A. V., & Huang, Y. (2003). The life course and residential mobility in British housing markets. *Environment and Planning A: Economy and Space*, *35*(2), 323–339. https://doi.org/10.1068/a3542

Coulter, R. (2013). Wishful thinking and the abandonment of moving desires over the life course. *Environment and Planning A: Economy and Space*, *45*(8), 1944–1962. https://doi.org/10.1068/a45314

Dovbischuk, T., & Kley, S. (2024). The call of the green: The role of green spaces in residential relocations across the life course in Germany. *Population, Space and Place*, e2810. https://doi.org/10.1002/psp.2810

Kearney, A. R. (2006). Residential development patterns and neighborhood satisfaction. *Environment and Behavior*, *38*(1), 112–139. https://doi.org/10.1177/0013916505277607

Kley, S. (2011). Explaining the stages of migration within a life-course framework. *European Sociological Review*, *27*(4), 469–486. https://doi.org/10.1093/esr/jcq020

Kley, S., & Dovbischuk, T. (2021). How a lack of green in the residential environment lowers the life satisfaction of city dwellers and increases their willingness to relocate. *Sustainability*, *13*(7), 3984. https://doi.org/10.3390/su13073984

Kley, S., & Dovbischuk, T. (2024). The equigenic potential of green window views for city dwellers' well-being. *Sustainable Cities and Society*, *108*, 105511. https://doi.org/10.1016/j.scs.2024.105511

Lachowycz, K., Jones, A. P., Page, A. S., Wheeler, B. W., & Cooper, A. R. (2012). What can global positioning systems tell us about the contribution of different types of urban greenspace to children's physical activity? *Health & Place*, *18*(3), 586–594. https://doi.org/10.1016/j.healthplace.2012.01.006

Liu, Y., Wang, R., Grekousis, G., Liu, Y., Yuan, Y., & Li, Z. (2019). Neighbourhood greenness and mental wellbeing in Guangzhou, China: What are the pathways? *Landscape and Urban Planning*, *190*, 103602. https://doi.org/10.1016/j.landurbplan.2019.103602

Mak, B. K. L., & Jim, C. Y. (2019). Linking park users' socio-demographic characteristics and visit-related preferences to improve urban parks. *Cities*, *92*, 97–111. https://doi.org/10.1016/j.cities.2019.03.008

Martin, L., White, M. P., Hunt, A., Richardson, M., Pahl, S., & Burt, J. (2020). Nature contact, nature connectedness and associations with health, wellbeing and pro-environmental behaviours. *Journal of Environmental Psychology*, *68*, 101389. https://doi.org/10.1016/j.jenvp.2020.101389

McEachan, R. R. C., Yang, T. C., Roberts, H., Pickett, K. E., Arseneau-Powell, D., Gidlow, C. J., Wright, J., & Nieuwenhuijsen, M. (2018). Availability, use of, and satisfaction with green space, and children's mental wellbeing at age 4 years in a multicultural, deprived, urban area: Results from the Born in Bradford cohort study. *The Lancet Planetary Health*, *2*(6), e244–e254. https://doi.org/10.1016/S2542-5196(18)30119-0

McMahan, E. A., Estes, D., Murfin, J. S., & Bryan, C. M. (2018). Nature connectedness moderates the effect of nature exposure on explicit and implicit measures of emotion. *Journal of Positive Psychology and Wellbeing*, *2*(2), 128–148.

Nisbet, E. K., Zelenski, J. M., & Murphy, S. A. (2009). The nature relatedness scale. *Environment and Behavior*, *41*(5), 715–740. https://doi.org/10.1177/0013916508318748

OECD. (n.d.). *What are equivalence scales?* Retrieved July 13, 2023, from www.oecd.org/els/soc/OECD-Note-EquivalenceScales.pdf

Permentier, M., Bolt, G., & van Ham, M. (2010). Determinants of neighbourhood satisfaction and perception of neighbourhood reputation. *Urban Studies*, *48*(5), 977–996. https://doi.org/10.1177/0042098010367860

Qiao, Y., Chen, Z., Chen, Y., & Zheng, T. (2021). Deciphering the link between mental health and green space in Shenzhen, China: The mediating impact of residents' satisfaction. *Frontiers in Public Health*, *9*, 561809. https://doi.org/10.3389/fpubh.2021.561809

Rosa, C. D., Profice, C. C., & Collado, S. (2018). Nature experiences and adults' self-reported pro-environmental behaviors: The role of connectedness to nature and childhood nature experiences. *Frontiers in Psychology*, *9*, 1055. https://doi.org/10.3389/fpsyg.2018.01055

Ruijsbroek, A., Droomers, M., Kruize, H., van Kempen, E., Gidlow, C. J., Hurst, G., Andrusaityte, S., Nieuwenhuijsen, M. J., Maas, J., Hardyns, W., Stronks, K., & Groenewegen, P. P. (2017). Does the health impact of exposure to neighbourhood green space differ between population groups? An explorative study in four European cities. *International Journal of Environmental Research and Public Health*, *14*(6). https://doi.org/10.3390/ijerph14060618

Tröger, J., Klack, M., Pätzold, A., Wendler, D., & Möller, C. (2016). *Das sind Deutschlands grünste Städte*. https://interaktiv.morgenpost.de/gruenste-staedte-deutschlands

Wolch, J., Wilson, J. P., & Fehrenbach, J. (2005). Parks and park funding in Los Angeles: An equity-mapping analysis. *Urban Geography*, *26*(1), 4–35. https://doi.org/10.2747/0272-3638.26.1.4

Wolch, J. R., Byrne, J., & Newell, J. P. (2014). Urban green space, public health, and environmental justice: The challenge of making cities 'just green enough'. *Landscape and Urban Planning*, *125*, 234–244. https://doi.org/10.1016/j.landurbplan.2014.01.017

Wu, W. J., Wang, M., Zhu, N., Zhang, W. Y., & Sun, H. (2019). Residential satisfaction about urban greenness: Heterogeneous effects across social and spatial gradients. *Urban Forestry & Urban Greening*, *38*, 133–144. https://doi.org/10.1016/j.ufug.2018.11.011

Zhao, Y., van den Berg, P. E. W., Ossokina, I. V., & Arentze, T. A. (2024). How do urban parks, neighborhood open spaces, and private gardens relate to individuals' subjective well-being: Results of a structural equation model. *Sustainable Cities and Society*, *101*, 105094. https://doi.org/10.1016/j.scs.2023.105094

6 Concluding remarks

While the analysis of public green spaces in cities is becoming increasingly relevant due to their beneficial impact on health (cf. Abraham et al., 2010; Coppel & Wüstemann, 2017; Honold et al., 2016; Stigsdotter et al., 2010; Wang et al., 2022), residential quality of life (cf. Kearney, 2006; Lee et al., 2016; Wu et al., 2020), and overall well-being (cf. Bertram & Rehdanz, 2015; Krekel et al., 2016; Zhao et al., 2024), a comparative analysis of different types of urban green spaces is rare (cf. Breuste & Artmann, 2020). Furthermore, little is known about which types of green spaces are used at different life course stages, or which socio-economic classes prefer certain green spaces in cities. In addition, there is limited understanding of which green spaces actually enhance satisfaction with urban nature and for which population groups. Based on a representative survey ($N = 1{,}840$) in two major German cities, these and other questions were investigated to better understand the importance of green neighbourhoods in cities.

It could be shown that the availability of public green spaces hardly differs across the analysed life course phases and socio-economic classes, but the use and motives for visiting these green spaces are different. While individuals in the young adult phase use urban green spaces less frequently, those in the family and senior phases spend the most time in urban green areas, which is consistent with previous research (Łaszkiewicz et al., 2023; Mak & Jim, 2019). Furthermore, there are strong differences across social classes, with higher social classes using public green spaces more frequently at least weekly. This frequency of use decreases with social class and is lowest in the lowest social class. Conversely, the least affluent social class spends the longest average time visiting urban green spaces.

The presence of private green spaces also influences how often people enjoy nature in their neighbourhood. For example, without a private garden or terrace, the use of parks increases in the family phase, and, in addition to parks, the use of waterfronts increases in the senior phase. Across all social classes, the frequency of visits to parks and waterfronts is higher when there is no private garden or terrace. The lack of a garden is also reflected in

DOI: 10.4324/9781003546146-7

satisfaction with nature, which is substantially lower for all respondents if there is no private garden.

Parks are used more frequently than other urban green spaces for socialising, both to meet friends and family and to play with children, which is consistent with previous research (Mak & Jim, 2019; Pinto et al., 2021). Individuals in the family phase are most likely to use parks to spend time with friends and family. They are also more likely than others to perceive parks as places to experience something exciting. The importance of nature enjoyment as a motive for park use increases over the life course, and peaks in the senior phase. In the young adult phase, parks are more frequently used as places for sporting activities than in other life course phases. People in the family and young adult phases spend more time in parks on an average visit than others. As far as differences across social classes are concerned, it is the lowest social class that uses parks least for sports activities, but more for socialising, which may explain why they spend the longest time in parks during an average visit. The two lower social classes are also more likely to use parks for relaxation, possibly because they have fewer resources for other relaxation opportunities. Future research could benefit from additional differentiation across various types of urban parks, as these can differ greatly in terms of infrastructure, size, vegetation cover, and facilities (cf. Breuste & Artmann, 2020).

Waterfront areas are used for motivations directly related to increasing mental well-being, such as relaxing, enjoying nature, or seeking exciting experiences. This use aligns with prior research indicating that the most common reason for choosing this particular type of green space is the need to experience the beauty of nature (Breuste & Artmann, 2020, p. 434). The young adult phase rarely visits waterfront areas for walking, but rather for sporting activities. Both the young adult and family phases visit waterfront areas more often for socialising than older individuals or peers without children under ten. The importance of enjoying nature in waterfront areas increases steadily over the life course, and becomes one of the two main reasons for using waterfront areas in the senior phase. In terms of social class differences, the lower social classes are more likely to use waterfront areas for mental well-being, such as enjoying nature or relaxing. In addition, the lower social classes use waterfront areas more often to spend time with children. The lowest social class spends the longest time in a typical visit to a waterfront area in good weather.

Woodland areas are primarily used for walking, which is consistent with the findings of previous studies (Breuste & Artmann, 2020, p. 434; Jensen & Koch, 2004). Both the young adult and senior phases use these areas more than others for walking, while the young adult and family phases use the wooded areas more than others for socialising. When it comes to sports or hobbies, people in the young adult and midlife phases use woodlands more frequently. Regarding social classes, the lowest social class is the least likely to use woods for walking. The more affluent social classes use woodlands more frequently to spend time with their children. The lowest social class spends the longest time in a typical woodland visit in good weather.

Fields and meadows are used most frequently for walking dogs compared to other green spaces, but least frequently by individuals in the senior phase. The young adult phase uses fields and meadows more often for exciting experiences and for hobbies. The family phase uses fields and meadows more frequently than others for activities with friends or family. In terms of social class, the lowest social class uses fields least often for sports or hobbies, and most often for activities with friends and family. This may explain why the lowest social class spends the longest time in fields and meadows when it comes to a typical visit to fields in fine weather.

Satisfaction with green spaces in the residential environment is highest in the family and senior phases, and lowest in the young adult phase, in line with previous research (Kearney, 2006). For the latter, the presence of parks and fields plays the most important role in their nature satisfaction – places where this life course phase is more likely than others to engage in sports, practise hobbies, or seek exciting experiences. For the family phase, there are no green spaces that are particularly favourable for increasing nature satisfaction. In the midlife phase, it is waterfront areas and woods, whereby the latter are used more often for sporting activities than in other life course phases. For the senior phase, waterfront areas are particularly important for nature satisfaction – the importance of enjoying nature in waterfront areas increases steadily over the life course, and becomes one of the two main reasons for visiting waterfront areas in the senior phase.

With regard to social classes, satisfaction with nature is relatively uniform across these classes. While the presence of waterfront areas is important for all social classes to increase nature satisfaction, parks remain insignificant. The presence of fields and meadows is important for the two middle socio-economic classes. The presence of woods is particularly relevant for the highest social class and for the two lower social classes.

Satisfaction with local nature tends to be lower among urban dwellers who do not have their own garden or terrace, across all life course phases and social classes. However, neighbourhood green spaces have been shown to increase nature satisfaction across demographic groups, even after controlling for the important predictor of the availability of private green spaces. The presence of a private garden is the most relevant factor in increasing nature satisfaction for city dwellers in the lowest socio-economic class.

The results of the analysis show that the relevance of green spaces in urban contexts should also be examined according to the type of green space. Furthermore, a distinction should be made among population groups, as both the usage preferences and the importance of these green spaces for overall nature satisfaction vary across both life course phases and socio-economic classes. Although the analysis of reasons for use in this book is already quite broad, to the author's knowledge it is one of the first attempts to produce a detailed analysis of urban green spaces based on a well-developed, randomised data collection. This disaggregated analysis should be useful for urban planning, helping to optimise the maintenance and development of green spaces, and ensuring that they meet the diverse needs of different urban populations.

References

Abraham, A., Sommerhalder, K., & Abel, T. (2010). Landscape and well-being: A scoping study on the health-promoting impact of outdoor environments. *International Journal of Public Health*, *55*(1), 59–69. https://doi.org/10.1007/s00038-009-0069-z

Bertram, C., & Rehdanz, K. (2015). The role of urban green space for human well-being. *Ecological Economics*, *120*, 139–152. https://doi.org/10.1016/j.ecolecon.2015.10.013

Breuste, J., & Artmann, M. (2020). Multi-functional urban green spaces. In J. Breuste, M. Artmann, C. Ioja, & S. Qureshi (Eds.), *Making green cities: Concepts, challenges and practice* (pp. 399–526). Springer.

Coppel, G., & Wüstemann, H. (2017). The impact of urban green space on health in Berlin, Germany: Empirical findings and implications for urban planning. *Landscape and Urban Planning*, *167*, 410–418. https://doi.org/10.1016/j.landurbplan.2017.06.015

Honold, J., Lakes, T., Beyer, R., & van der Meer, E. (2016). Restoration in urban spaces: Nature views from home, greenways, and public parks. *Environment and Behavior*, *48*(6), 796–825. https://doi.org/10.1177/0013916514568556

Jensen, F. S., & Koch, N. E. (2004). Twenty-five years of forest recreation research in Denmark and its influence on forest policy. *Scandinavian Journal of Forest Research*, *19*(S4), 93–102.

Kearney, A. R. (2006). Residential development patterns and neighborhood satisfaction. *Environment and Behavior*, *38*(1), 112–139. https://doi.org/10.1177/0013916505277607

Krekel, C., Kolbe, J., & Wüstemann, H. (2016). The greener, the happier? The effect of urban land use on residential well-being. *Ecological Economics*, *121*, 117–127. https://doi.org/10.1016/j.ecolecon.2015.11.005

Łaszkiewicz, E., Kronenberg, J., Mohamed, A. A., Roitsch, D., & De Vreese, R. (2023). Who does not use urban green spaces and why? Insights from a comparative study of thirty-three European countries. *Landscape and Urban Planning*, *239*, 104866. https://doi.org/10.1016/j.landurbplan.2023.104866

Lee, S. M., Conway, T. L., Frank, L. D., Saelens, B. E., Cain, K. L., & Sallis, J. F. (2016). The relation of perceived and objective environment attributes to neighborhood satisfaction. *Environment and Behavior*, *49*(2), 136–160. https://doi.org/10.1177/0013916515623823

Mak, B. K. L., & Jim, C. Y. (2019). Linking park users' socio-demographic characteristics and visit-related preferences to improve urban parks. *Cities*, *92*, 97–111. https://doi.org/10.1016/j.cities.2019.03.008

Pinto, L., Ferreira, C. S. S., & Pereira, P. (2021). Environmental and socioeconomic factors influencing the use of urban green spaces in Coimbra

(Portugal). *Science of the Total Environment*, *792*, 148293. https://doi.org/10.1016/j.scitotenv.2021.148293

Stigsdotter, U. K., Ekholm, O., Schipperijn, J., Toftager, M., Kamper-Jorgensen, F., & Randrup, T. B. (2010). Health promoting outdoor environments – associations between green space, and health, health-related quality of life and stress based on a Danish national representative survey. *Scandinavian Journal of Public Health*, *38*(4), 411–417. https://doi.org/10.1177/1403494810367468

Wang, R., Feng, Z., & Pearce, J. (2022). Neighbourhood greenspace quantity, quality and socioeconomic inequalities in mental health. *Cities*, *129*. https://doi.org/10.1016/j.cities.2022.103815

Wu, W., Dong, G., Sun, Y., & Yun, Y. (2020). Contextualized effects of park access and usage on residential satisfaction: A spatial approach. *Land Use Policy*, *94*. https://doi.org/10.1016/j.landusepol.2020.104532

Zhao, Y., van den Berg, P. E. W., Ossokina, I. V., & Arentze, T. A. (2024). How do urban parks, neighborhood open spaces, and private gardens relate to individuals' subjective well-being: Results of a structural equation model. *Sustainable Cities and Society*, *101*, 105094. https://doi.org/10.1016/j.scs.2023.105094

Index

For Product Safety Concerns and Information please contact our EU representative GPSR@taylorandfrancis.com
Taylor & Francis Verlag GmbH, Kaufingerstraße 24, 80331 München, Germany

www.ingramcontent.com/pod-product-compliance
Lightning Source LLC
LaVergne TN
LVHW010939110826
845149LV00013B/2682
* 9 7 8 1 0 3 2 9 0 1 0 0 8 *